KT-593-657

Contents

Foreword

This is the first time that the East Midlands will have had the opportunity to study work by Paul Klee, long recognised as one of the truly great artists of the 20th century. That this exhibition has been made possible has been due to the kindness and generosity of Paul Klee's son, Felix in lending us so many works and who welcomed me into his home with such warmth and hospitality. Also to the Trustees of the Victoria and Albert Museum and Fischer Fine Art for lending works.

We were further helped by the financial support of the Visiting Arts Unit of Great Britain and the aid of the Pro Helvetia Foundation of Switzerland and I thank Kenneth Pearson of the V.A.U. and Benôit Junod, First Secretary, Cultural Affairs at the Swiss Embassy for arranging this support. I would also like to express my appreciation for Her Majesty's Government for insuring the exhibition under the terms of the National Heritage Act.

I would like to thank David Phillips of Manchester University for his encouragement and help in selecting the works; Dr. Richard Verdi of York University for giving up so much of his time to help us, offering valuable advice and for writing the catalogue introduction; and the many other people who have helped to prepare the exhibition, including Dr. Trudy Berger, Elizabeth Boa and Eva Grauberg for translating an often difficult text; Nick Alfrey, Krzysztof Ciezskowkzsi, Wendy Barrett, Ann Buddle, Albert Haynes, Jeremy Hunt, David Jones, Howard Kendall, John Robson, Barbara Smith, all the staff of Nottingham Castle Museum, and finally my husband Eddy Keon for his forebearance and patience during the setting up of the exhibition.

Michaela Butter
Exhibitions Officer,
Castle Museum.
April 1983.

Exhibition Dates
Nottingham Castle Museum 29 May - 31 July
Museum of Modern Art, Oxford 7 Aug - 18 Sept

Introduction – Felix Klee

To this day the memory of Paul Klee is clearly before me. Until 1916 Klee was in charge of the household duties in Munich, which meant also the not always easy task of educating his son Felix. My mother Caroline Sophie Elisabeth, known as Lily, had to earn our daily bread by giving piano lessons, that is why she couldn't possibly attend to the daily running of the house. Paul took over and rose to the occasion with the utmost skill.

I was often ill – five times I had pneumonia, then tonsillitis, bad colds, and jaundice; that was the normal run of things. Klee nursed me with touching patience and dedication, took a clean paintbrush instead of a wooden spoon for stirring the semolina pudding he prepared for me and improved it with cinnamon and sugar or raspberry syrup. He also took an interest in my homework and in my daily drawing and painting activities.

My earliest childhood memory dates from 1912. We spent the summer holidays in Beatenberg above Lake Thun in the Hotel Beau Séjour, which belonged to my great aunt Louise. On our departure for Berne the whole family walked to the mountain station of the funicular railway. On the way a snake crossed the dusty road in front of us. We all froze and admired its wavy tracks. The snake disappeared under some nearby bushes. After we had continued on our way, Klee turned round several times, quite attentively. I asked my father the reason for his behaviour. Klee replied: 'There are snakes who put their tail into their mouth and follow you like a hoop.' Again and again I turned round to see whether the snake was following us.

In 1916 Klee began making figures for me for a Punch and Judy show (so-called Kasperl-figures). All in all he made fifty of these up to 1925 – thirty of which are still in existence. The costumes were made by Sasha von Sinner, a friend of the family, who later married the painter Ernst Morgenthaler. Klee made most of the heads out of plaster of Paris; later on he used a variety of materials like matchboxes, plugs, wood, cattle bones and papier maché. As far as the choice of characters was concerned Klee always complied with my wishes: Kasperl, his friend Sepperl, Mr. and Mrs. Death, the Devil and his grandmother, the policeman, and the crocodile. In the small apartment a large picture frame was hung in between the door leading from the bedroom to the dining room. On this picture frame Klee stuck bits of material – a sort of collage made out of materials from the mending drawer in the chest which was most efficiently looked after by Lily.

And how did Klee watch over my drawing and painting activities? He kept everything I ever produced, looked after it as though it was his own work, and wrote on it the captions that I invented. Klee is quoted as having mentioned this fact in the following words: 'The pictures my little Felix has painted are better than those which often dribbled through my own brain'. In 1914 Klee often left me with Kandinsky who lived nearby, where, I could draw and paint to my heart's content. From that moment on my work was deeply influenced by the Russian's rich world of colour. To this day I often think of this remarkable painter and man with awe and admiration. Many themes aroused my interest like the war which had just broken out, the theatre, the feverish thoughts during my illnesses, the yearly journeys from Munich to Berne, technical matters in connection with a vehicle called the 'Dinterin' – you could travel with it anywhere, wherever your fancy took you, now to the North Pole, now to the South Pole.

I often watched Klee at work, when, for instance, like an alchemist he was busy preparing his printing in the kitchen, or busy with his culinary art, his perfect playing of the violin, his painting, or above all his drawing. In the small flat in München-Schwabing, Ainmillerstrasse 32, at the back, there were three small rooms, the living room, the bedroom for the three of us, and the slightly larger music-room, where Lily gave her piano lessons and where Paul and Lily played sonatas almost every evening. Modern music? Far from it! – Bach, Handel, Haydn, Mozart, Beethoven, Schubert, occasionally daring a step forward to Brahms and Schumann. There was only gaslight, an old fashioned stove, a long dark corridor, and an equally long corridor leading to the lavatory, where there was a carefully selected library, a bath which had to be heated by coal, a servant's room which was also used a guestroom, a big kitchen where my father pitched his tents, and a big balcony which served as a fridge in winter. Twice a year there was a fair in Munich called the Auer Dult. There were merry-go-rounds and shooting stalls and above all a Kasperltheater (a Punch and Judy show), where my father sent me with plenty of coins so that he could be left in peace to go to the nearby flea market to buy some picture frames – with or without paintings or photos – for 2 Marks each. After 2 hours' delightful performances with Kasperl, Death, and the Devil, Klee – much to my regret – collected me to go home and help him carry his frames.

Klee would often sit as the only spectator in front of my puppet theatre, smoking his pipe, with Fritzi, the tom-cat, on his lap, delighting in each scene of broad comedy in this popular entertainment. I made his works come to life in performance. Apart from the puppets, he also made the scenery, as for instance a beautiful village, a collage with a striking church spire. I often think even today of these leisure hours of my father and of how they reverberated in his superb work.

On various occasions I had to act as amanuensis, accompanying the master on his wanderings, just to help carry the utensils. Once it was the North Cemetery or the Aumeister or the Würm Canal in Milbertshofen. Klee made little boats for me which I could sail on the water. I can also still remember a splendid railway station which he constructed out of bits of cardboard, putting in rooms, inscriptions, windows, and a signal box. Later Klee often told me of the pranks and anecdotes in which I figured so prominently. There was a drawing to which I gave the title 'Uncle Fritz?' My answer: 'He has just excused himself and left the room'. Another time I met him on the Friedrichstrasse. I pretended to be a locomotive and raced towards him at full speed. He stood there, his arms open to stop me. My reaction: 'Don't touch me. I am terribly hot'. and then, from 1916-1918 came the visits together with Lily to the pioneer and later lance-corporal Klee in Landshut, Schleissheim and Augsburg. My imagination got new food-for-thought. I often think of how understanding Klee was in dealing with my wild temper. Then in 1919, in his studio in the little baroque Werneck Castle, called Suresnes, neighbour to Lahusen, the musician, and Hans Reichel, the painter who in 1919 offered Ernst Toller a hideout after the "Räterepublik", the Bavarian part of the German Revolution. Or, in 1920-22 the holidays in Possenhofen. Klee loved fishing, but one day the railings by the bathing huts collapsed and he fell, fishing tackle and all into Lake Starnberg. Lily and I were at home in fisherman Gebhardt's apartment when we heard strange noises – plash, plash, plash! – on the stairs. He was wet through, we took his clothes off and hung them near the oven to dry.

In October 1921, at the age of 13 years and 9 months, I was admitted as the youngest pupil and 'gifted' painter to Master Johannes Itten's class in the Bauhaus in Weimar. Klee had been working there as a Master for a year. I remember that splendid period of my jeunesse dorée with great joy. After a preliminary course I learned woodwork which Klee called my 'military service'. And when in 1925 I had passed the exam, Klee asked: 'What do you want to be? Don't become a painter, your future wouldn't be too promising – choose something else for your main job – after all, you can paint as much as you like in your spare time'. My reply: 'In that case I would like to choose the theatre!' Klee: 'Then you choose that!'

From this vantage point at the end of my seventy fifth year I can look back over a wealth of memories of my wonderful youth. Klee's versatility is apparent from the 10,000 works which he left behind.

Much basic analytical work has been done on Klee's art by those more qualified than I. From my own point of view I simply wanted to describe Paul Klee, the man, my father, and how he behaved towards a growing child. There are many connections with his art from start to finish. Many a mystery is yet to be discovered.

I would like everybody who looks at Klee – be it at easy or difficult themes – to come with open eyes and open hearts.

Felix Klee
Berne, December

Translated from: Paul Klee, Briefe an die Familie 1893-1940, ed Felix Klee, Cologne, Du Mont Buchverlag, 1979 vol II

Single Sheet from the Year 1908

Answer to printed Questions

Your favourite qualities in a man?	A good all-round education and intelligence
Your favourite qualities in a woman?	Health and good manners
Your favourite occupation?	Seeing
What is your idea of happiness?	To be successful in one's work
Which job seems to you the best?	The one that takes most of your talent
Who would you like to be other than yourself?	A cat in my house
Where would you like to live?	Nowhere without friends
In which epoch would you like to have lived?	—
Your idea of bad luck?	Not to be able to work
Your main trait of character?	To be factual, to deal with things, my things
Your favourite authors?	The short ones
Your favourite painters – and sculptors?	Goya, Manet
Your favourite composers?	Bach, Mozart, and Beethoven
Your favourite colour – and flower?	All, if they are well blended/well painted
Favourite heroes in history?	—
Favourite heroines in history?	—
Favourite characters in poetry?	The demoniac ones
Your favourite names?	Lily
Which historical characters can't your bear?	The insincere ones
Which errors would you forgive first and foremost?	Printing errors
Your pet aversion?	To have to talk a lot
What are you frightened of?	The jury
Favourite dish and drink?	Good red wine
Your temperament?	It depends on my mood

Lebenslauf

Ich bin am 18. Dezember 1879 zu München-
-Buchsee geboren. Mein Vater war Musik-
lehrer am Kantonalen Lehrerseminar Hofwyl,
und meine Mutter war Schweizerin. Als ich im Frühjahr
1886 in die Schule kam, wohnten wir in der
Länggasse in Bern. Ich besuchte die ersten vier
Klassen der dortigen Primarschule. Dann
schickten mich meine Eltern ans Städtische
Progymnasium, dessen vier Klassen ich absolvierte,
um dann in die Literaturschule derselben Anstalt
einzutreten. Den Abschluss meiner allgemeinen
Bildung bildete das Kantonale Maturitätsexamen,
das ich im Herbst 1898 bestand.

Die Berufswahl ging äusserlich glatt
von Statten. Obwohl mir durch das Maturitäts-
zeugnis alles offen stand, wollte ich es wagen,
mich in der Malerei auszubilden und die Kunst-
-Malerei als Lebensaufgabe zu wählen. Die
Realisierung führte damals — wie teilweise auch
heute noch — auf den Weg ins Ausland.
Man musste sich nur entscheiden zwischen Paris
oder Deutschland. Mir kam Deutschland

The first page of an application for Swiss Citizenship which Paul Klee wrote in 1940 (translated in full on the opposite page).

"I was born December 18, 1879, in Münchenbuchsee. My father was a teacher of music at the Cantonal Teachers' College of Hofwyl; my mother was Swiss. When I started school in the spring of 1886, we lived in the Länggasse, Berne. I attended the first four grades of the local primary school, followed by four years at the municipal *Pro-gymnasium.* I then entered the *Literarschule* of the *Gymnasium,* and passed the Cantonal examinations, graduating in the fall of 1898. This concluded my general education.

Choosing my profession proved easy enough, outwardly at least. While every career was open to me by virtue of my graduation certificate, I decided to study painting and to devote my life to art. In order to realize this goal, I had to go abroad (the same would be true of many young Swiss artists today), either to Paris or to Germany. I felt more strongly drawn to Germany, and chose to go there.

That is how I came to the capital of Bavaria, where on the advice of the Art Academy I started out at the private Knirr Art School. I practiced drawing and painting there, and before long was able to enter the class of Franz Stuck at the Academy. After three years of study in Munich, I broadened my experience by a year of travel in Italy, which I spent mostly in Rome. And then I had to settle down to digesting what I had learned, and to make it the point of departure for independent work. For this programme of quiet work I returned to Berne, the home of my youth; the fruits of my stay there were a number of etchings done between 1903 and 1906, which even then attracted some notice.

During my Munich years I had made many friends, including the woman who is my wife. Since she was professionally active there, I decided – for what seemed to me an important reason – to move back to Munich in the fall of 1906. I was slowly making a name for myself as an artist; and Munich, a center of art and artists at that time, offered significant prospects of professional advancement. Except for three years of military service, when I was stationed at Landshut, Schleissheim, and Gersthofen, I remained settled in Munich until 1920. At the same time, I maintained my link with Berne, returning every year to the home of my parents for a summer holiday of two to three months.

In 1920 I was appointed to the faculty of the Bauhaus in Weimar. I taught there until 1926, moving then to Dessau, the new location of the school. Finally, in 1930, I received a call to the Prussian State Academy in Düsseldorf, to be in charge of a painting class. I welcomed this appointment; it permitted me to confine my teaching to the field I knew best. I taught at this Academy from 1931 to 1933.

The political upset in Germany had its impact on the fine arts, too, constricting not only my freedom to teach but the free excercise of my creative talent. Since I had by then achieved an international reputation as a painter, I felt enough assurance to give up my salaried position and to devote all my efforts to my own creative work.

The question of where to settle down for this new phase of my life answered itself. I never really lost touch with my home town; now I was strongly attracted to it again. I have been a resident here ever since. My one remaining wish is to become a citizen as well."

Berne, January 7, 1940   (signed) Paul Klee

Reproduced from Paul Klee, by W. Grohmann (publisher W. Kohlhammer, Stuttgart).
By kind permission of Lund Humphries Ltd., London

Paul Klee — the teacher

Translated from Aus der Malklasse von Paul Klee, Berne, 1957 by Petra Petitpierre.

Exhibitions

The director of the Basle Museum came to select some pictures for an exhibition in Basel. If the truth be known, I don't like parting with my pictures. I feel almost abandoned, especially when they take a lot of them away. They are all my children and I am very fond of them, even of the weaker ones. But I always hide one or two for myself – for myself and no one else. I am so happy whenever I possess drawings and watercolours which no one has ever seen. They are the ones that really belong to me.

Whenever an artist has his first exhibition he attaches great importance to it. I did too. But later on, looking back, the first exhibition is the least important.

Paul Klee shows his own works

In art we must pursue just such an aim as in nature, but we are unable to free ourselves completely from the example of nature. The sum total of experiences in nature makes up our knowledge. We are no longer naive; we know that the function to be performed gives rise to the form. This tempts many artists to try something comparable, purely in analogy to natural creation. Instead of making something which will vie with nature, they make something which says: this is just like nature. Anyone who works in this receptive way has nothing to do with us of course.

By way of comparison

One can often compare a picture by saying: 'It is like . . .'. That would be a simile for it. But all similes are ambiguous, and something else might equally do.

It is something poetic – I say poetic, not literary – that almost speaks by way of simile. A simile, as if there were some fear of saying explicitly how it is. A simile by Homer: Morning is like someone scattering rose petals. You say a lot more like that. The same may be said about our metaphorical art. It must be added that it is always a question of creative freedom and not of a definite connection.

Often things are almost veiled in a mist, as though something very harsh were being conveyed softly.

Regarding the realm of colour

Colouring always has something mysterious about it, which is not easily grasped, this extraordinary enigma can only be solved in the mind. Colours are the most irrational thing in painting. There is something suggestive about them – a suggestive power. Unbroken colour, intensity of colour is especially appealing.

The old masters dealt with colour last in their pictorial structures, we, on the other hand, want to be colourists first and foremost.

We can only approximate to the colours of the spectrum as absolute colour values. What pure red, blue, or yellow, etc. is, we can at best only sense (psychically).

Abstract

It's quite interesting that in spite of all abstraction things remain real. This difference can often be sensed within abstract art. Does an abstraction ever go so far that the real disappears, that it dematerialises? Sometimes one could almost think that something had been painted from nature, from a model so to speak, a wire model or something of that kind. This type of abstraction obviously excites one's curiosity. But can this be called abstract?

It is after all not necessary for everything to be crystal clear, but if one investigates something thoroughly, the question arises: how is this, and what is that? One can imagine a mixture of the clear and the unclear, keeping strictly to the proportions, so that the effect is convincing. But they would have to express something special. This sort of reality (when it is shown in a picture) only means that it is something copied and coloured in.

The abstract in a picture is absolute and as such may only be sensed – experienced deep down. Similarly, the abstractness of a piece of music or a poem does not lie in the theoretical construction but is intrinsically there and can always be sensed. Therefore it may be wrong to speak of abstract art at all. This kind of abstraction, which is constructed according to theory, is contrived, made. There is no possibility of an end result; either a certain something exists or it does not. Let us say therefore that the absolute in expression exists or that it does not. Abstract art can be very concrete and non-spiritual.

The old masters did not tell about the abstract, they made it.

The Artistic

In the end everything passes away and what has remained from earlier times, what remains of life, is the spiritual, the spiritual in art. Or let us simply call it the artistic. In everything we do the demand for the absolute remains constant. We must not so confine ourselves to the concrete object that we neglect the pictorial image. By all means let us do as we please, but as regards the final total form in an absolute sense a solution must be found. If a picture is good it must be inwardly satisfying independently of the content of what is represented.

Formerly when I was asked about a picture I would simply not know what it represented, I had not seen the object depicted. Now I include the content so that I generally do know what is being represented.

This only goes to support my experience that what matters in the end is harmonisation in an absolute sense. It is not a matter of deciding what to do, but of deciding what our activity can achieve in doing justice to each individual case. Whatever one does, whether it is achieved in a moment or in years of work, everything demands the whole person.

Death

Death is not something terrible, I came to terms with it long ago. Who knows after all which is more important, life now or the life to come? Perhaps the other life is more important, but that is something of which we have no clear knowledge. I shall die gladly when I have created a few more good works.

Paul Klee (1879-1940): an introduction to the exhibition

Paul Klee's art is so rich and varied in both content and style that no exhibition, however large, could do full justice to its remarkable range. Nevertheless, the present exhibition – which is drawn entirely from the collection of his son, Felix Klee – offers a balanced and representative selection of works from nearly all phases of his career and includes many of his finest pictures. In an output which totals nearly 10,000 paintings, drawings, and prints – the majority of them titled, dated, and numbered by the artist himself in his exemplary catalogue of works – gaps and omissions are inevitable. However, the examples included here do provide a good indication of the wide emotional range of Klee's art, of his inexhaustible inventive powers, and of his constant search for new technical and stylistic means of expressing his ideas. Moreover, they afford a rich opportunity to appreciate the sincerity and seriousness of an artist who is too often linked in the popular imagination merely with the realms of wit and high comedy. From the mystical landscapes of 1917-20 included here, and from the outstanding group of late works, it may be seen that Klee was also an artist of undoubted power and profundity – and of much darker moods. It is to be hoped that the exhibition will succeed in winning new admirers for this great modern master, who has never enjoyed the high reputation in Great Britain that he does in Europe or North America and who still remains poorly represented in the national collections.

Probably the initial impression conveyed by a room hung with Klee's pictures is that of their sheer beauty in both colour and design; and there can be no doubt that in both of these respects Klee remains one of the most gifted and resourceful of all modern painters – and also one of the most immediately appealing. But what of his subjects? Initially, these may appear more baffling and lead one to conclude that Klee was a mere fantasist who inhabited a world of dreams and fairy-tales which bears little relation to our own. Although it would be foolish to deny that a streak of whimsy and fantasy informs many of his more light-hearted creations, in his most considered pictures – that is to say, those which well up from the deepest regions of his being – Klee often aims to put us in touch with a reality much greater than that which meets the eye and creates a world which runs parallel to our own rather than divergent from it. In these the artist poetically rearranges the features of a landscape, or the landmarks of the cosmos itself, in order to introduce us to those hidden truths about nature which remain forever invisible and which Klee himself regarded as 'ultimate things'. This was Klee's ambition from the very start of his career and finds its most memorable expression in the oft-quoted opening sentence of his *Creative Confession* of 1918: 'Art does not reproduce the visible, it makes visible'.

From the discussion which follows – and more importantly, from the works themselves – it will be seen that Klee's art seeks to make visible a truly encyclopaedic range of subjects and themes – from the emotions of man to the mysteries of nature, and from the laws of architecture to those of music. For all the poetry and inventiveness of his art, however, Klee remains essentially a realist in his desire to lay bare the invisible secrets in the world about him in his art. Moreover, he surveys this world with a perpetual sense of wonderment and surprise that is truly infectious and succeeds in reawakening in us that same sense of wonder and delight which accompanied our own first sight of things. This freshness and beguiling simplicity in Klee's art lends to it an immediate appeal and has often led him to be seen as a child's painter. But if Klee's gaze focuses upon creation with the innocent eye of the child, it does so with the hindsight of the sage. Re-enchanting the world about us, it constantly strives to make us see it anew – and with deeper insight. For this reason probably the most important prerequisite to a fuller enjoyment and appreciation of Klee's pictures is the willingness to recapture one's innocence while still retaining one's wisdom.

Klee was that rare phenomenon among artists – a true polymath. Born into a musical family, he himself became an accomplished violinist and, between 1902-06, even played professionally with the municipal orchestra of Berne. With his departure from that city Klee continued to perform regularly in duet and chamber recitals, often accompanied by his wife, the pianist Lily Stumpf. Throughout his life, too, music was to remain not only an absorbing interest but a deep source of pictorial inspiration. In addition, Klee was a serious student of both the natural and physical sciences and maintained a lively interest in architecture and the theatre. All of these pursuits may likewise be felt in his art and account for something of both its discipline and its diversity. In his earliest works, however, Klee found himself most powerfully attracted to the world of nature, which he recognised from the start as 'the power that maintains'. Initially regarding himself primarily as a landscapist, he devoted his first series of paintings to views of the countryside around his native Berne, among them the 1902 *Autumn Landscape with a Lake and Trees* (1). Although Klee considered these pictures tentatively painted 'technical experiments' and was later to exclude them from his catalogue of works, many of them already reveal a sensibility finely attuned to the more poetical features of the scene – and , in the case of this *Autumn Landscape,* to its haunting stillness, its fragility, and its insubstantiality. Thinly and nervously painted, this little picture testifies to the young artist's determination to transcend the bounds of either realism or impressionism in order to uncover a more spiritual side to nature.

One year before painting this picture, in October 1901, Klee journeyed to Italy, where he remained for seven months, visiting most of the major artistic centres and immersing himself in the study of the art of antiquity and of the old masters. Awed and at times intimidated by much that he saw there, Klee admitted to finding very little in the noble style of the past that seemed relevant to his own age and sought a different means of expressing his own ideas about humanity. 'This is why I am again all on the side of satire', he confessed in his *Diaries*. This leaning towards satire in his treatment of the human figure is apparent in the series of fifteen major etchings which Klee completed in 1903-05 and which he regarded as the earliest works in his career to show true originality – in short, as his 'Opus One'. Unlike the landscape just discussed these are works drawn solely from the imagination and dedicated to exploring (and exposing) the pretences and hypocrisies of human behaviour. From an early age Klee acknowledged that, even in the realm of the plastic arts, he was 'at bottom . . . a poet'. And such key early etchings as his *Virgin in a Tree* (2) of 1903, one of the first and most famous of this group of 'sour' prints, reveals the extent to which he was willing to distort the forms of the living world in order to put them at the service of his idea. That idea is best described to us by Klee himself in an entry in his *Diaries,* written shortly after completing this etching: 'The beasts (the birds) are natural and paired. The lady wants to be something special through virginity, but doesn't cut an attractive figure. Critique of bourgeois society'.

In addition to its satirical content and impressive technical skill, Klee's *Virgin in a Tree* also commands our attention as an early example of one of the most distinctive features of his artistic vision – one which he was to employ with increasing subtlety and refinement to the end of his career. This may best be described as his poetical feeling for nature and is immediately apparent in this etching on the level of a simple visual pun: namely, that between the gnarled and atrophied form of his virgin and that of the tree upon which she reclines. Klee was forever given to uncovering features common to the most diverse creations in nature and, already with his visit to Italy, he had observed that the linear principles of certain tree trunks were not unlike those of the human body. Turning this discovery to his own poetical ends, he here creates an image of barrenness and sterility in nature by comparing the unfruitful woman with the unfruitful tree and contrasting them both with the paired and mating birds. Nor can one fail to notice the ingenious way in which Klee permits his tree to reveal to us something of his virgin's thoughts, and even of her belated desires. As her legs part a prominent gnarl in the tree itself reminds us of precisely that portion of her own anatomy which she wishes to deny. Moreover, if one retraces the outlines of the tree trunk in this etching one will gradually discover in it the form of a leering human face looking towards the left – of a rejected suitor in disguise, perhaps, who has here returned to haunt the virgin's thoughts.

Satire of a different kind marks Klee's *The Pianist Struggling* (3) of 1909. In his catalogue of works Klee described this drawing as a 'comical caricature sheet on modern music'; and it is not hard to sympathize with this pianist as he faces a chaotic and cacophonous musical score by one of the avant-garde composers of the day. Ironically contrasted with it is the lyre-like music stand upon which it rests, its elegance and simplicity evoking the purer music of a bygone age. Shackled to the pedals of his piano and unceremoniously seated upon a chamber pot, Klee's harassed pianist takes on the form of a plucked chicken whose neatly aligned vertebrae resemble the key holes of a clarinet – until, that is, they converge upon the chamber pot and deliver his decisive verdict on the excesses of the new music. Although Klee was eventually to find himself in sympathy with some of the music of his own age, his lifelong preference was for the great masters of the baroque era and of the Viennese classical school – Bach, Mozart, Haydn, Beethoven, and Schubert – none of whose scores resemble the barrage of notes which here confronts his desperate pianist.

From the works just discussed it may be seen that Klee's earliest creative efforts oscillated between studies from nature and those from the imagination and that in the latter of these especially he sought to communicate a poetical idea. In the years around 1910, however, Klee returned to the study of nature in the hope of evolving a style which would gradually permit him to express his ideas about it in a manner which was both wholly original and truly pictorial. Klee himself defined this goal as one of bringing 'architectonic and poetic painting into a fusion' – in other words, of creating works in which content and style were indissolubly bound and the poetry of his chosen subject was revealed in the very handling of the forms themselves. Among his most important strides forward of these years are *House and Field* (4) of 1909, the self-portrait of the same year, *The Artist at the Window* (5), and the 1910 *Girl with Jugs* (6). In all three of these the forms appear pressed towards the picture plane as though to reaffirm the two-dimensional nature of the design. Now no longer an illusion of reality, Klee's pictures strike us instead as genuine constructions. Further reinforcing this effect in all three instances are the vehement brushwork and the rhyming and repeated shapes and colours which often depart from the bounds of mere description to bestow a purely abstract logic upon the scene.

For all their importance in his career, each of these works is essentially a homage to an older master whose influence Klee is known to have felt during these years. In *House and Field* the surging bands of paint which build up the terrain recall the art of Van Gogh, whose works Klee had seen in a large exhibition in Munich in 1908. Although Klee confessed to finding Van Gogh's pathos alien to him, he admired his predecessor's ability to free his line from a concern with the appearance of things in order to allow it to impart an overall harmony to his pictures. And this aspect of Klee's admiration is apparent in his own *House and Field,* where the swirling brushwork serves less to evoke the charged emotional atmosphere of Van Gogh's pictures than their taut, rhythmic coherence.

A year after his introduction to Van Gogh's art Klee saw eight pictures by Cézanne at the Munich Sezession and immediately recognised in this master 'the teacher *par excellence'*. This new influence is apparent in Klee's *The Artist at the Window* of this same year, which is a study from life presumably done with the aid of the window reflection itself, since Klee was in fact left-handed. Now confining himself almost entirely to a range of sepia tones which are subtly modulated throughout the design Klee seeks an even firmer integration of space and surface here than in his *House and Field*. Light and shade, patterned and plain areas are all interwoven into a design whose abstract qualities threaten almost to usurp attention from its subject. Although the monochromatic palette which Klee employs here is one rarely associated with Cézanne, the minute gradations of tone, the faceted brushstrokes, the geometric firmness of the design, and the absence of linear boundaries between the forms all call to mind the style of Cézanne's maturity.

In *Girl with Jugs* Klee reintroduces clear, black outlines into the design, which shape and contain the forms of the still life objects and of the girl herself and thereby add greatly to the tectonic strength of the whole. Further enlivening the impression are the vividly contrasting reds, violets, and blues out of which he builds his entire scene, the whole rendered with a freshness and spontaneity which perfectly complements the cheekiness of his human figure. Both of these devices recall the art of Matisse, whose works were also to be seen in Munich in 1909. Of the three works of these years exhibited here, *Girl with Jugs* most successfully harmonises space and surface, line and colour, and solid and void into a coherent whole. In addition to achieving this through a series of rhythmically repeated colours which decorate both the jugs and the rouged cheeks of the young girl, Klee integrates his design through an ingenious series of visual rhymes which are again reminiscent of Matisse. Thus the swelling and pointed shapes of the jugs mirror those of the head and shoulders of the girl herself, while at the lower right the neck and spout of one of Klee's jugs appears to mimick this figure's own neck, nose, and eye.

For all its boldness and vitality, Klee's *Girl with Jugs* remains a transitional work in his career in its clear indebtedness to the art of another master and in its somewhat obvious formal and colouristic rhymes. Moreover, along with the two works which precede it in the exhibition, it still remains fundamentally tied to the depiction of a precise motif in nature. Thus, although it is an impressively architectonic picture, it is not a particularly poetical one; that is to say, one in which the plastic means of picture construction – line, form, tone, and colour – are made to reveal to us those invisible truths in the world about him which Klee had long sensed and sought to express in his art.

Klee's breakthrough to a style of true pictorial originality which could then be placed at the service of his ideas came with two crucial encounters – one with art and the other with nature – which took place in 1912 and 1914 respectively and whose result was the style that we immediately recognize as 'Klee'. The first of these was a visit to Paris in 1912 where Klee encountered the works of the Cubist painters, whose desire to penetrate beneath the surface of nature to discover its essential truths had gradually led them to reduce their pictures to an intricate network of intersecting lines and planes interspersed with motifs suggestive of the real world – but of a world which now had to be recreated in the viewer's mind from a handful of pregnant clues provided by the artist. In the formal innovations of Cubism Klee at last discovered a means of achieving a rigorous structural unity in his own pictures; and in such works of the following years as *Wings for 'The Anatomy of Aphrodite'* (8) or *Architecture with the Red Standard* (9) he likewise limited himself to a geometric scaffolding of planes of pure colour – to bricks or bands of paint which might build up the entire design and ensure its formal logic.

With this new and more architectonic means of constructing his pictures Klee gradually found himself able to release colour itself from the role it had served in such works as *Girl with Jugs* and to permit it a greater variety and autonomy within the design. No longer employed in a repeated and somewhat predictable manner, it could now be permitted to sing out with an independent voice in his pictures. This new freedom in his handling of colour – one which is fully apparent in the 1917 *With the Rainbow*(10) or the 1919 *Landscape with the Setting Sun* (17) – owes itself to the second of Klee's crucial encounters of these years. This was his brief visit to Tunisia in the spring of 1914, where the clarity and intensity of the light and atmosphere of this exotic land proved to be an overwhelming experience – one which led Klee to free his own pictorial colour from the position of subservience (and the slight quality of murkiness) it had retained in his early works and to endow it with an unparalleled power and purity. 'Colour and I are one', he exclaimed of this magical moment in his career, 'I am a painter'.

Klee's growing confidence in the handling of both form and colour during these decisive years may be seen from a comparison of the three works of 1913-15 exhibited here. The earliest of these is *Card Game in the Garden* (7), which depicts Klee's young son Felix, his sister Mathilde, and his wife Lily. In this modest little watercolour, which is painted on a sheet of writing paper folded down the middle, the forms are as summarily rendered as in the 1909 *Artist at the Window*. But whereas that work had relied upon a limited range of repeated tones to ensure its overall unity, the 1913 watercolour is held together by a rigorously symmetrical composition and by a sequence of repeated hues which unite the two halves of the design. To be sure Klee still confines himself here to a colour harmony of reds, pinks, and blues in the somewhat tentative manner of the *Girl with Jugs*. But, given the firmer underlying structure of his design, it is noteworthy that he no longer feels compelled to resort to the somewhat obvious formal and colouristic rhymes of that earlier picture.

To move from Klee's *Card Game in the Garden* to his *Wings for 'The Anatomy of Aphrodite'* is suddenly to have the scales fall from one's eyes. In this, the first post-Tunisian picture in the exhibition, Klee opens up the full rainbow of his palette to include the most vividly contrasting hues – from red to green, yellow to violet, orange to brown, and black to white. The effect is breathtaking, with all of these colours now calling to one another from one sheet to the next instead of merely mirroring or echoing themselves in the somewhat contrived manner of the *Card Game*. Rather, Klee employs these bold, answering hues as equal weights in his designs and, in so doing, renounces all his previous inhibitions in the realm of colour and firmly proclaims to us that he is 'a painter'. The two sheets which make up this brilliantly coloured work form the wings of a triptych whose central portion is now lost. In their thin and soaring forms they may be seen as appropriate to a goddess who rose from the sea or even as evocative of the shafts of her son Cupid's arrows.

In *Architecture with the Red Standard,* which was completed later the same year, Klee has tightened and bounded the contours of his planes of colour to achieve a stricter pictorial organization. As in the two preceding works, the separate halves of the design are broadly complementary and are here united by the centrally-placed flagpole, which rises above the surrounding streets and houses. In its rigorously interlocking planes and colours, this design – which was originally conceived as an oval composition – possesses a clarity and finality which look forward to Klee's works of the 1920s.

If the works just discussed show Klee's increasing mastery in the handling of the architectonic aspects of pictorial composition the pictures which follow them in the exhibition demonstrate the many, more poetical uses to which he eventually applied these discoveries and direct our attentions to the most diverse facets of life itself. Typical of these is the 1919 *Rocky Landscape with Palm Trees and Fir Trees* (15), in which Klee reintroduces hieroglyphic linear elements into the architecture of his picture and suddenly bewitches the multi-coloured terrain. Simple shapes brimming with life now stand for suns, moons, trees, and rainbows without in any way imitating the forms of these objects as they appear in nature. Instead, Klee prefers to evoke rather than to describe; and in this case he evokes a rugged and labyrinthine realm which is visited by suns and decorated with trees but which man may ascend, it seems, only with the help of a ladder. An enchanting – and enchanted – world which runs parallel to our own, forever recalling it without ever recording it.

Few generalizations can be made about Klee's choice of subjects in his mature years; for, by his own admission, Klee felt 'at home with all things over, on, and under this earth' and, at one time or another, most of these things found their way into his pictures and gave to his art the quality of a cosmic picture-book. In a handful of works – among them *The Great Kaiser armed for Battle* (21) of 1921 or the soulful *Young Proletarian* (13) of two years earlier – Klee reminds us that he lived through one of the most turbulent periods in European history and chooses unashamedly topical themes. But much more often his pictures are concerned with more timeless subjects – with the make-believe world of the theatre or opera house, the charmed world of the fishes and flowers, the inexhaustible domain of human life, or simply with those unending cycles of nature and of the cosmos against which all else must ultimately be seen. In all of these realms Klee seeks a position of crystalline detachment before his subjects and creates works which often strike us as cool and distant – and at times appear like so many conjuring tricks from an undisclosed source. Avoiding an undue concern with his own passions and feelings, Klee prefers to survey the entire domain of existence from a cosmic vantage point in the manner of his figurative self-portrait of 1919, *Lost in Thought* (14). In this the artist presents himself as a meditative and disembodied presence floating weightlessly on the page with all the serenity and authority of a Buddhist idol. Withdrawn and rapt in contemplation, he seems to exist above the vicissitudes of a normal human existence and to inhabit an omniscient realm. No longer a seeker after truth, he is instead a true seer.

Klee's crystalline detachment before his subjects is nowhere better seen than in his 1918 watercolour *Sexual Awakening of a Youth* (11). In this a young boy suddenly enters manhood, his head crowned with a halo of dawning recognition and his raised right arm vigorously proclaiming both his new-found knowledge and his burgeoning sexuality. Plainly visible to the left of the design are the bearers of this revelation – a virile bull, its one eye fixed vigilantly upon us, who jealously guards his chosen mate, her coyly downcast eyes and lashes rhyming with her distended udder and teats. As so often in his works, Klee here takes as his theme one of life's central experiences and presents it to us in a manner which seems both wholly impersonal and intensely poetical. As it happens, however, the imagery of this sheet may be directly related to an episode in Klee's own early life. At the age of only two or three years Klee had a dream about the family maid in which her sexual organs were revealed to him. 'They consisted', he later noted, 'of four male (infantile) parts and looked something like a cow's udder'. Thus, faithful to his childhood dream even in maturity, Klee still found the key to sexual understanding in the image of a cow's udder when he painted his *Sexual Awakening of a Youth*. But far from infusing this work with the imprint of his own early psychic experience Klee endowed it with an aura of mystery and magic which raises it to a truly universal realm.

In other works of these years Klee turns his attentions to landscape and creates enchanted visions of the most diverse moods and moments in nature. Thus, in *With the Rainbow* of 1917, he evokes through the abstract manipulation of planes of pure colour that longed-for moment when the arc of the rainbow appears above the horizon and signals the end of a storm. One has only to look at this rainbow again, however, to realize that it may also be read as a large eye – perhaps the benevolent eye of the creator himself looking down upon the landscape and blessing it with the gift of the rainbow. In *Growth in an old Garden* (16) of two years later Klee creates a design whose lacy delicacy calls to mind the finest embroidery. In this the yellow disk of the sun hovers weightlessly above an overgrown garden where dense, intricate hatchings and dimly glowing hues serve perfectly to evoke a time-honoured realm. And in *'E', Fragmentary Watercolour* (12) of 1918 Klee transports us to the mythical land of *E* and allows the elements of his landscape to orbit around the large form of this letter and to rhyme with its straight and pointed contours. Is this the land of *E*-nigma? One can never be sure in so mysterious an artist as Klee. But what is certain is that Klee's use of this letter differs fundamentally from the uses to which the Cubist painters had put similar motifs in their pictures. For Picasso and Braque such letters had served simply as reminders of the real world and often stood in place of the most mundane objects of that world – posters, newspapers, etc. When Klee introduces such elements into his pictures, however, he invariably bestows upon them a poetic meaning which transports us out of our own world and into a wholly imaginary realm.

The unending cycles of nature form the subject of two further landscapes of these years – the 1919 *Landscape with the Setting Sun* (17) and *Cemetery* (18) of a year later. In the former Klee literally lowers the sun into the bottom right of the sheet with the aid of a large black arrow which signals the end of the day. In a few moments the small red moon next to it will rise, night will fall, and the right-hand margin of Klee's picture will come to resemble the left-hand edge. The planes of blue and green pressing towards the right will expand to fill the awaiting space, the black rectangle at the upper right of the sheet will grow to touch the top in the manner of its counterpart at the left, and perhaps even the patch of yellow next to this rectangle will unfurl to reveal the prominent black rays displayed by its counterpart on the left. Through all of these devices Klee invites us to complete his picture and to relive that magical moment at the end of the day when the warm orb of the sun sinks below the horizon and the veil of night descends.

In his *Cemetery* Klee alludes instead to the broader cycles of death and rebirth in nature – a favourite theme of the German romantic painters of the early nineteenth century and also of Klee himself. One has only to contemplate the simple shapes which inhabit this landscape to realize that some stand for crosses and others for trees and that the dividing line between the two (especially at the upper right) is often very thin. Through this disarmingly simple visual equation Klee reminds us of those new lives which draw sustenance from old lives in this cemetery setting – in short, of the ever-renewing powers of nature itself.

In 1921 Klee was appointed to the staff of the Bauhaus, which had been founded by the architect Walter Gropius, who sought to bring about a synthesis between the fine and applied arts and to instruct artists and craftsmen alike in the fundamental problems of design and construction. The curriculum was divided into a preliminary course, which was devoted to a basic grounding in the laws of form, colour, and materials, and to a number of more specialized workshops. In his twelve years at the Bauhaus – first in Weimar and then in Dessau – Klee directed the stained glass workshop and taught courses in weaving and painting. In addition, he contributed to the all-important preliminary course, which afforded him a unique opportunity to reflect upon the methods and materials of his own craft. The result of these teachings was a series of lectures and pedagogical notebooks which remain amongst the most significant contributions to twentieth century art theory by any major painter. Throughout these Klee appears to be primarily concerned with problems of pictorial form and design – with what might be called the architecture of a picture – and, not surprisingly, many of his own works of these years likewise reveal a rigour and discipline of design and construction which makes the paintings of the preceding decade still appear somewhat improvisatory.

This is immediately apparent if one compares the 1922 *Separation in the Evening* (23) with the thematically related *Landscape with the Setting Sun* of 1919 just discussed. In the later work Klee evokes the fall of night with a purity and simplicity which seem truly irreducible. Graduated bands of colour moving from violet to blue descend upon the horizon to meet the dying rays of the sun, which are themselves rendered as a rising sequence of hues from red to yellow. In the centre of the design two arrows prepare to touch, the long, weighty arrow of night bearing down upon the slowly sinking arrow of the day, which must now yield to it. Closely related in style to this work is the 1923 *Three Towers* (26), where a prismatic sequence of blues and pinks build up the spires of Klee's three towers, soaring heavenwards with a delicate and ethereal effect which calls to mind stained glass and may owe something to Klee's own experiences in directing this workshop at the Bauhaus. But far from being the product of mere pedagogy, his *Three Towers* inhabits a realm of pure poetry. Finally, in *Star-Bound* (27) of the same year the realms of heaven and earth meet as Klee's human figures join hands with the stars as though with the bearers of their destiny. Such a work may seem pure fantasy — or at most fanciful astrology — until one remembers that Klee himself sought a creative position which would place him 'on a star among stars'.

Other works of this period in a similarly constructivist vein reveal Klee's interest in perspective and the importance accorded to architecture generally in the Bauhaus curriculum. Among these are the 1921 *Transparent Perspective (With the Pavilion)* (19) and *Italian City* (31) of 1928, the latter recalling the rugged and sunbaked cityscapes of southern Italy, which Klee had visited in the same year. But perhaps the supreme example of his researches into the realms of form and colour during the Bauhaus years are such 'magic square' compositions as *City Picture (With the Red Dome)* (25) of 1923. In this, planes of pure colour centred around two pairs of complementaries — red and green, and black and white — fill the entire picture and create a harmony which may justly be likened to a kind of visual music. On the right large areas of muted colour and a narrow tonal range build up the edifice of the dome-capped city, while on the upper left brighter and smaller squares gently rise above these, like hovering clouds. Despite the economy and simplicity of Klee's means in such pictures they remain works of pure intuition and of a refined sensibility. This is above all evident in the treatment of the squares of colour themselves, which are painted with loose, breathing edges which endow them with all the vitality of living things.

If Klee's so-called 'magic square' pictures represent the purest examples of his explorations into the realms of form and colour, other works of these years serve to remind us of his continuing interest in the most diverse range of pictorial subjects. Among these is the demonic *Actor* (24) of 1923, which may draw its inspiration from the famous Bauhaus theatre or even from the puppets and puppet theatres which Klee was designing for his young son Felix during these years. Other works draw their motifs from the world of nature, which was always to form the single greatest sourcebook for Klee's imagery. Two examples are *Rose Wind* (22) of 1922, with its playfully punning flower and colour, and *Fish in Circle* (29), which was begun in 1926 and reworked ten years later in the broad and solemn style of Klee's last years. Even within the same period of his life, however, Klee was capable of working in a variety of styles, as may be seen from his delicately painted *Hermitage* (28) of 1925. In this the artist creates an impression of stillness and secrecy appropriate to his subject by isolating his scene in the middle of the sheet, as though literally surrounding it with silence. So sensitive is Klee's understanding of the relationship between subject and treatment here, too, that the landscape is drawn in a nervous and hesitant line which seems almost stitched into the paper and perfectly evokes a realm of hermetic seclusion.

Two further works of these years demonstrate the purely poetical ends to which Klee could turn even the most abstract exercises in pictorial construction. These are *Fugue in Red* (20) of 1921 and *Harmony of the Northern Flora* (30) of six years later. Although both of these works would appear to be concerned with the harmonization of a series of forms and colours, the titles which Klee gave to them call to mind more precise themes from those two other worlds he knew so well, music and nature. In *Fugue in Red* Klee creates the visual equivalent of an eighteenth century fugue by a composer such as Bach through a graduated sequence of shapes and colours distributed in rows across his picture as though on a musical score. Like a musical score, too, Klee's design demands to be read from left to right and top to bottom. Only in this way will one discover that the artist has also presented us with an astonishingly accurate account of a musical fugue. Such works typically consist of a subject and counter-subject, which are here rendered as curvilinear and rectilinear shapes, the former being subtly varied and developed into pitcher shapes, circles, and pointed ovals, and the latter into squares, rectangles, and triangles. In addition Klee also alludes here to certain of the favourite devices employed by composers to vary and develop their own ideas in a fugal composition. Among these are the techniques of inverting a single musical line (cf. Klee's inverted triangles at the bottom right); of playing a line backwards or in 'retrograde motion' (cf. the shifting axes of the ovals at the top and bottom right); and of inverting the position of two lines which are played simultaneously – a practice known as 'invertible counterpoint'. The last of these is apparent in Klee's treatment of the squares and pitcher shapes in the centre of his picture, the former of which are first 'heard' above the pitcher shapes and then (at the far right) below them.

If Klee's *Fugue in Red* reveals his remarkable knowledge of the laws of musical composition, *Harmony of the Northern Flora* demonstrates his equally astute understanding of the laws of nature. Here, through the mere manipulation of the basic elements of his art – line, form, and colour – Klee evokes the essence of vegetative existence in a temperate realm. With firm black lines containing his individual areas of varied but muted colour, he miraculously reminds us of the rigours and restraints exercised upon those blossoms native to climates where there is always a slight chill in the air.

During the early 1930s Klee's ceaseless inventiveness led him to evolve a variety of new styles and techniques which further extended the formal and expressive possibilities of his art. In one of these – represented in the exhibition by *World Port* (38) and *Two Women in a Forest* (35), both of 1933 – Klee applied thin layers of pigment to the surface of his sheet with a palette knife, creating delicate ribbons of paint which could be made to resemble weaving patterns. In *World Port* the result is an intricate weft of vertical and horizontal strokes which recall that eternal dialogue between earth and sky or land and sea hinted at by Klee's title. In such a work Klee creates an art of pure relations which calls to mind Mondrian's pier and ocean studies of 1914-15, which are likewise exercises in an intricate linear counterpoint. In *Two Women in a Forest,* on the other hand, Klee employs this technique to create a dense and entangled forest setting which threatens to ensnare these two lost figures and, in its ominous mood, prefigures the art of Klee's final years. Like the many doors which lead nowhere in his maze-like *Opened* (37) of this same year, there would appear to be no way out of this forbidding forest for Klee's two hapless wanderers.

Yet another technical innovation which Klee had first used in the 1920s is represented in the exhibition by the 1934 painting, *The Invention* (40), in which paint has been sprayed onto the surface of the work with an atomizer. The result is an unusually atmospheric and impersonal effect – one which seems devoid of all handiwork and is ideally suited to the mysteriously glowing head of the inventor in this picture, whose shadowy presence lurks behind his invention and whose alert and piercing gaze quietly proclaims to us 'Eureka!'.

But by far the most important of Klee's technical innovations of this period was a style of painting in minute dots of colour which are applied in serried rows over a coloured ground and frequently combined with linear elements. These mosaic-like pictures are often referred to as divisionist or 'pointilliste', though they in fact owe little to the pointillism of Seurat except in their use of the dot technique. With their resulting sparkle and shimmer these remain amongst the most luminous of all Klee's creations — works in which a disembodied and impalpable light fills the scene and creates a vibrant and otherworldly impression. Ideally suited to this technique is Klee's *Pastor Kol* (34) of 1932 — solemn, meditative, and himself seemingly disembodied, his thoughts forever turned to spiritual things. In *Emacht* (32) of the same year, the dot procedure adds to the weightlessness and immateriality of a mobile-like construction which derives its name from the letter and number it was assigned in Klee's oeuvre catalogue for 1932 — M8 (Em-acht). In both of these works Klee appears to us at his most cool and detached, creating works in which that most rarified and elusive of all pictorial elements — light — has become the chief concern of his art.

But this detachment was to be short-lived, for with Klee's dismissal from Germany by the Nazis in 1933 and with the onset of his fatal illness two years later his art took a decidedly more personal turn. Resettled in Berne for the remainder of his life, Klee embarked upon the most productive phase of his entire career, creating nearly one-third of his total output during his last seven years. This achievement becomes even more remarkable when one considers that the degenerative skin disease which was eventually to kill him (sclerodermia) was one which slowly and insidiously robbed him of his physical powers — and above all of his manual dexterity. In the face of this growing deterioration throughout Europe and within himself, Klee evolved a late style of the utmost seriousness and simplicity in which bold, monumental forms fill the picture field and a mood of sombre gravity prevails. In these valedictory works — at once so powerful and portentous — Klee addresses us with a depth of insight and an intensity of feeling which are arguably unequalled by the late works of any other major painter of this century and which call to mind instead the visionary late styles of certain of the most venerated old masters.

Although the range of subjects to be met with in Klee's late art is no less extensive than that of the preceding years, the dominant impression conveyed by these is one of a deep pessimism which increasingly veers towards tragedy and makes it easy to see why one critic was moved to describe all of Klee's late works as 'Variations on the theme — "The End — period".' In keeping with this more introspective approach to his art, Klee's subject matter itself often reveals to us his primal obsessions and his darkest fears. In short, this hitherto most detached and crystalline of painters now becomes a deeply personal — and often openly autobiographical — one.

Two such examples exhibited here are *Struck from the List* (39) and *Head of a Martyr* (36), both of which were painted in 1933 — the year of Klee's own enforced flight from Germany. In the former a Semitic figure gazes sorrowfully out at us, her head scored with a condemning black cross which seems to mark her as an outcast and already portends the myriad victims of the holocaust. In the latter Klee depicts an aged and defeated martyr destined for his final suffering — a kind of Veronica's veil for the 1930s, grim, ravaged, and more suitable for scourging than for succouring. Scarcely less intense in its pathos is Klee's *Suffering Fruit* (41) of the following year. In this a single fruit-like form ominously fills the picture space. Although its stem and calyx suggest that it is a kind of dessert fruit, its shape more closely resembles that of an ordinary potato. And, as if this were not humiliation enough, its skin bears all the marks of an insidious and disfiguring blight. In the middle of its body a large downcast eye poignantly conveys both its pain and its shame and (like the lone eye of the Cyclops) redoubles our pity through its pathetic singleness.

In his more straightforward depictions of nature, too, Klee often imparts a dark and threatening mood to his late pictures, as for example in his doom-laden *Menace* (47) of 1938. Yet another landscape of these years – the 1939 *Night is Falling* (50) – may be usefully compared with the two earlier representations of this theme in the exhibition, *Landscape with the Setting Sun* and *Separation in the Evening.* In contrast to the fantasy and enchantment of the former or the cool rationality of the latter, Klee's late treatment of this theme is pervaded by pale, lunar yellows and ominous greys, with the entire paint surface being worked up in a turbulent and agitated manner. Strewn across this surface are the landmarks of the terrain, adrift like so much flotsam and jetsam on the rising waters of the Flood. Far from evoking merely the end of the day, this lugubrious little picture seems to portend the end of the world. Less sombre – but no less mysterious – are the two garden pictures exhibited here, *Autumn Garden Picture* (33) of 1934 and *Twilight Blossoms* (56) of 1940. In the latter of these especially Klee's sturdy and simple blossoms appear to be endowed with a primeval power as they glow with a strange incandescence against the night sky.

Two further works included here unite the emotions of man with those of nature. These are *Figure in a Garden* (42) of 1937 and *The Grey One and the Coast* (46) of the following year. In the latter a watchful human presence looks out over a jagged coastline as though alerted by a signal of distress. In the former neither the beauty of the colour nor the simplicity of the design can entirely divert us from the broken and mournful human figure imprisoned within this garden setting and weighed down by a large, ripe fruit preparing to fall from an overhanging branch. Although religious imagery is rare in Klee's art, it is hard not to see this combination of images as a stark reminder of the consequences of original sin – especially when one considers Klee's own circumstances during these years. Yet another indication that this theme was one of Klee's final obsessions is the large number of serpents to be found in his late pictures. The imagery of the example exhibited here – the 1939 *Fence and Snake-lines* (52) – requires no explanation, though it is worth noting that images of both terror and confinement are often to be met with in these last works.

Although Klee's many late depictions of the human figure are too diverse in type and mood to be easily categorized, the majority of them too seem to be burdened by the heavy hand of fate. This may even be seen in such comparatively light-hearted works as *Abstract Ballet* (45) of 1937 or *A Child's Game* (51) of 1939. In the former Klee creates a kinetic design out of a group of mechanized dancers who turn somersaults and pirouettes as they traverse the canvas; while in the latter Klee depicts a young girl out skipping with her pet rooster. For all the innocence of this picture's title and subject, however, it is hard not to detect something joyless in the proceedings. It is perhaps less of a romp than a ritual.

In both *In the Meadow* (43) of 1937 and *Mother and Child* (48) of the following year Klee chooses another traditionally joyous theme and infuses it with sorrow. Although the figure group in the latter openly recalls that of a Madonna with the infant Christ, the pale, chalky hues and the fateful solemnity of the expressions already seem to prefigure the Pietà. Perhaps this explains the prominent fruit-like form which again weighs down upon this figure and the ominous M (for *Mord* – or murder?) incised on the forehead of her child. In his *Weeping Woman* (53) of the next year Klee confronts us with an image of inconsolable human misery which likewise calls to mind a mourning figure at the foot of the cross. Further intensifying this mood are the deathly hues and the weathered paint surface, which suggests a figure ravaged not only by grief and suffering but by time itself. On the opposite end of the emotional scale is one of the most harrowing of all Klee's late pictures – *A Double-Crier* (49), also of 1939. In this the artist presents us with a menacing image of terror and demonic possession. Rolling, mobile features, prong-like hair, and saw-like teeth here combine with a clashing colour chord of yellow, orange, red, and violet to emit a shriek of sheer visual anguish which is blood-curdling. As so often in his late pictures Klee here appears to us to be exorcising the demons of his own final imaginings.

These demons take on one further – and even more fateful – form in Klee's many late works depicting monstrous beings or objects which seem slowly and ominously to be metamorphosing into other forms of life. Such hybrid types abound during these years and suggest a new awareness on the artist's part of the most irrational elements and impulses in nature. Occasionally – as in *The Bastard* (55) of 1939 – Klee's late hybrids strike us as humorous and even lovable, in the way so often elicited by mongrels. But more often they appear deeply disquieting and seem to foretell the collapse of the balance of nature itself. Thus, in *Face of a Vase* (44) of 1937 and *Wave Sculpture* (54) of 1939 inanimate objects suddenly appear to us endowed with the qualities of life and, with their swelling and tumorous curves, seem capable of engulfing all of normal existence in their wake.

This theme of the perversion – or even overturning – of the balance of nature finds its fullest expression in the late untitled *Still Life* (59) of 1939-40, which was left unfinished at Klee's death and remains one of his most complex and mysterious creations. With its basic repertoire of figures, flowers, and planets set against an impenetrable black void scored with fateful crosses, this picture immediately announces to us that we are confronting the dying artists's final thoughts on the order of existence. By any reading of the picture, these thoughts would appear to be deeply distressing and profoundly pessimistic. For, as Klee here depicts them, the living things of this world – in this case plants and flowers – appear dead or thwarted in their attempts to beget new life, with the broken forms of his blossoms now strewn over a table-top as though over a grave-stone or swimming in their vases as though more drowning than drinking. Indeed, when viewed upside down the cut flowers in the vase at the upper left of this picture become acrobatic schoolgirls riding on a unicycle underwater and, thereby, literally drowning. In contrast to all of this, however, the creations of inanimate nature now appear endowed with almost obscene powers of growth, procreation, and self-assertion. Jugs and pitchers sprout arms, breasts, faces, and phalluses and suddenly stake a claim for themselves among the most vigorous and dynamic of nature's creations. In such a guise they also become amongst the most threatening and perverted, especially when one recalls that their thrusting and saluting gestures were also a hall-mark of the militant youth of the 1930s and would bring in their wake not the promise of new life but only the certainty of mass death.

This topsy-turvy view of existence is brought forth even more mercilessly in the drawing of an angel at the bottom of Klee's picture. Like the plants and flowers it accompanies it remains a true contradiction in terms – a heavenly being which here appears earth-bound, anguished, and seemingly strangled, presiding over a world in which living things wither and die and the non-living suddenly acquire ominous life.

Premonitions of death also mark two of Klee's very last works, *The Cupboard* (57) and the so-called *Angel of Death* (58). In the former the artist creates one of his most claustrophobic late images and also one of his most bitterly ironic. Nominally a cupboard, this sealed black box contains not utensils but a raging fire. A furnace, then – or even an inferno. In his *Angel of Death* Klee presents us with a vision which can only be likened to the dying strains of his own Requiem. Here a gauzy, spectral being holds a silent vigil at the edge of a bottomless black hole. Monstrous, polyp-like trees haunt the landscape, and the whole scene appears bathed in an eerie and unearthly light – a pale and waning light which itself appears about to be snuffed out. Unsigned and untitled, this ghostly image, which seems conjured forth from the edges of the nether-regions themselves, was among the effects found in Klee's studio at his own death, on the 29th June 1940.

Dr. Richard Verdi, 1983

I cannot be grasped in the here and now
For I live just as well with the dead
As with the unborn
Somewhat closer to the heart of creation than usual
But far from close enough

Does warmth come from me? Coolness?
That cannot be discussed beyond all heat.
Most distant I am most devout,
Here in this world often rather malicious:
These are but nuances of one and the same thing.
The priests are just not devout enough to see it.
And they become a little annoyed, the scholars of Holy Writ.

"A Jotting" Paul Klee (1916)

Autumn Landscape with a Lake and Tree
Herbstlandschaft mit See und Bäumen

25

Girl with Jugs
Mädchen mit Krügen

26

**Wings for the Anatomy
of Aphrodite**
Flügelstücke zur
Anatomie der Aphrodite

With the Rainbow
Mit dem Regenbogen

Sexual Awakening of a Youth
Sexuelle Erkenntnis eines Knaben

Growth in an old Garden
Wachstum in einem alten Garten

Landscape with the Setting Sun
Landschaft mit sinkender Sonne

31

**The Great Kaiser armed
for Battle**
Der grosse Kaiser, zum
Kampf gerüstet

Separation in the Evening
Scheidung Abends

City Picture with the Red Dome
Städtebild, rot grün gestuft,
mit der roten Kuppel,
vier Elemente

34

Three Towers
Drei Türme

35

Star Bound 1923
Sternverbundene

36

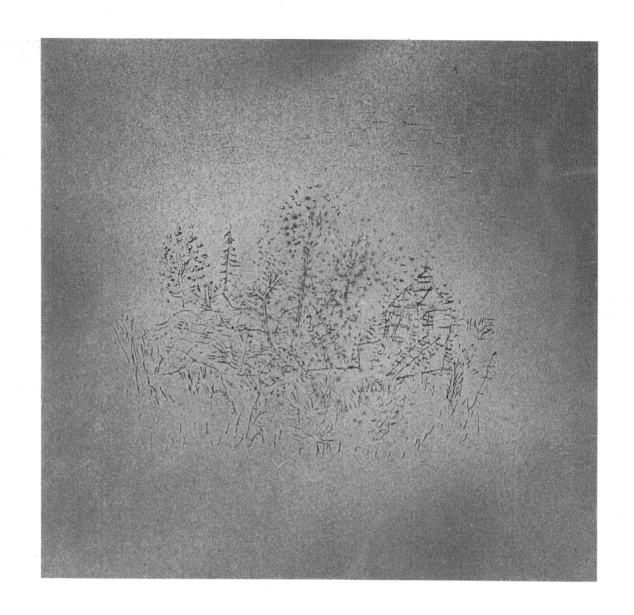

Hermitage
Einsiedelei

Fish in Circle
Fische im Kreis

38

Harmony of the Northern Flora
Harmonie der nördlichen Flora

39

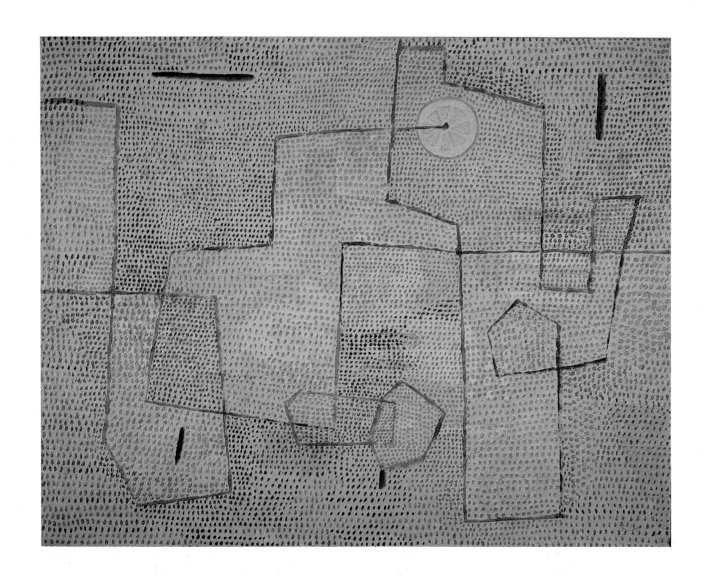

M8
Emacht

40

The Invention
Die Erfindung

Figure in a Garden
Figur im Garten

Night is Falling
Es dämmert

A Child's Game
Ein Kinderspiel

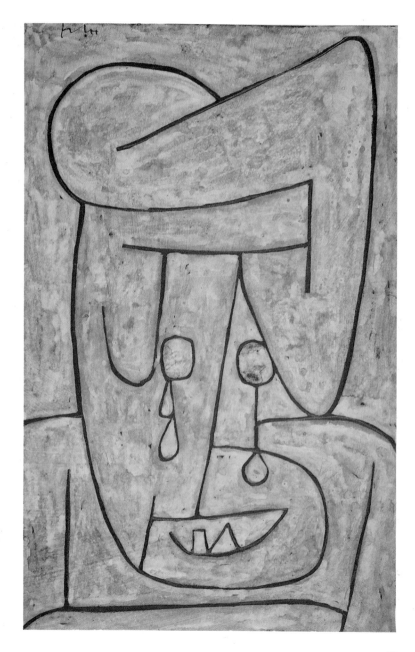

Weeping Woman
Weinende Frau

Twilight Blossoms
Dämmer-Bluten

46

Angel of Death
Der Todesengel

47

Still Life
Stilleben

1

2

3

4

1 **Autumn Landscape with a
  Lake and Tree.**
  (Originally untitled) 1902
  Herbstlandschaft mit See und
  Baümen. Oil on board 28.5 x 32.5
  Unsigned

2 **Virgin in a tree**
  1903.2 Jungfrau im Baum
  Etching State 3. Etching on zinc
  23.3 x 29.7 Signed bottom middle

3 **The Pianist Struggling**
  1909.1 Der Pianist in Not.Witzblatt,
  Karikatur auf die moderne Musik
  Watercolour on French Ingres paper
  16.7 x 18 Signed bottom left

4 **House and Field**
  1909 (Originally untitled)
  Haus und Acker. Oil on Board
  32 x 21.5 Signed at top

Paul Klee developed his own reference system
for dating pictures. The earlier works have the
year and number beside it, later on, he replaced
the year with a letter code, both systems are
quoted here. All works are in chronological
order.
All measurements in centimetres.

5 **The Artist at the Window**
1909.70 Der Zeichner am Fenster
Ink and wash, coloured chalk on
paper 30 x 23.7 Signed bottom right

6 **Girl with Jugs**
1910.12 Mädchen mit Krügen
Oil on brown board 35 x 28
Signed top right

7 **Card Game in the Garden,
Berne, with Felix, Mathilde,
Lily Klee**
1913.201 Kartenspiel im Garten
Watercolour on writing paper
21 x 28 Signed top left

8 **Wings for the Anatomy
of Aphrodite**
1915.48 Flügelstücke zur Anatomie
der Aphrodite. Watercolour on
chalk ground. Ingres paper
23.4 x 19.4 Signed top left

5

6

7

8

9

10

11

12

9 **Architecture with the Red Standard**
1915.248 Architectur mit der Roten Fahne. Watercolour and oil on chalk ground. 31.5 x 26.3 Signed top left

10 **With the Rainbow**
1917.56 Mit dem Regenbogen Watercolour on chalk ground 18.6 x 22 Signed top right

11 **Sexual Awakening of a Youth**
198.111 Sexuelle Erkenntnis eines Knaben. Watercolour on aircraft canvas with coloured plaster ground 22.7 x 24 Signed top left

12 **"E", Fragmentary Watercolour**
1918.199 "E", Fragmentarisches Aquarell Watercolour on chalk ground 22 x 18.1 Signed top left

13

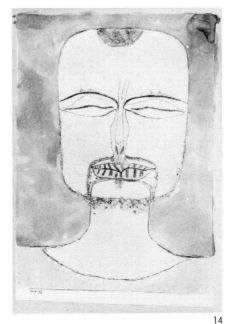

14

13 **Young Proletarian**
   1919.111 Junger Proletarier
   Oil on board 25 x 23.5
   Signed bottom right

14 **Lost in Thought**
   (Self portrait) 1919.113
   Versunkenheit – Selbstportrait
   Coloured lithograph with
   watercolour 25.6 x 18 Unsigned

15 **Rocky Landscape with Palm
   Trees and Fir Trees**
   1919.155 Felsenlandschaft mit
   Palmen und Tannen. Oil on board
   42.5 x 51.5 Signed bottom left

16 **Growth in an old Garden**
   1919.169 Wachstum in einem
   alten Garten. Watercolour on
   chalk ground 15 x 21
   Signed bottom left

15

16

17

18

19

20

17 **Landscape with the Setting Sun**
   1919.247 Landschaft mit sinkender Sonne
   Watercolour on chalk ground on French
   Ingres paper 19.9 x 26.1 Signed top right

18 **Cemetery**
   1920.79 Friedhof. Oil on old canvas
   17 x 25.5 Signed bottom left

19 **Transparent Perspective
   (with the Pavilion)** 1921.55 Transparent
   und Perspectivisch, mit dem Pavillon
   Watercolour on Fabriano paper 25.5 x 29.5
   Signed bottom right

20 **Fugue in Red**
   1921.69 Fuge in Rot. Watercolour on
   Canson paper 24.3 x 37.2 Signed bottom left

21

22

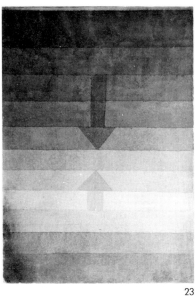

23

24

21 **The Great Kaiser armed for Battle**
1921.131 Der grosse Kaiser, zum Kampf
gerüstet. Oil and watercolour, plaster ground
laid on linen finished paper 43.5 x 28
Signed top left

22 **Rose Wind**
1922.39 Rosenwind. Oil mounted on sized
Dutch-made paper 42 x 48.5
Signed bottom left

23 **Separation in the Evening**
– diametrical gradation in blue,
violet and yellow 1922.79
Scheidung Abends, diametralstufung aus
blauviolett und gelborange. Watercolour on
French Ingres paper 33.5 x 23.5
Signed bottom left

24 **Actor**
1923.27 Schauspieler. Oil on black and
white on wrapping paper 46.5 x 25
Signed top right

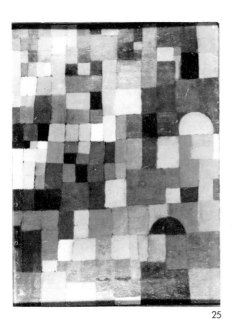

25

26

25 **City Picture with the Red Dome**
1923.90 Städtebild, rot grün gestuft, mit der roten Kuppel, Vier Elemente. Oil on paste board 46 x 35 Unsigned

26 **Three Towers**
1923.101 Drei Türme
Watercolour on French Ingres paper 32.8 x 23
Signed bottom right

27 **Star Bound**
1923.159 Sternverbundene
Watercolour 32.5 x 48.5
Signed bottom right

28 **Hermitage**
1925 S 2(92) Einsiedelei
Pen and watercolour on German Ingres paper
27.2 x 28.7 Signed top right

27

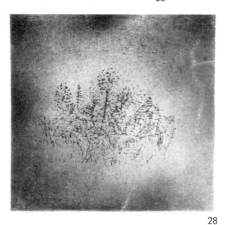

28

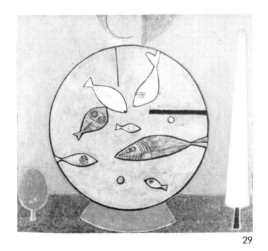

29

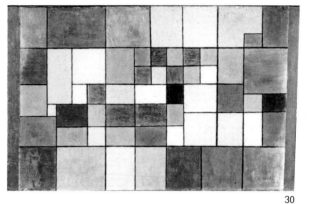

30

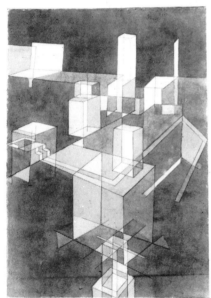

31

29 **Fish in Circle**
   1926 E (nil) 140 Fische im Kreis
   Oil, tempera on linen mounted on
   cardboard 42 x 43
   Signed top left

30 **Harmony of the Northern Flora**
   1927 E4(144) Harmonie der
   nördlichen Flora. Oil on cardboard
   41.5 x 67 Signed bottom right

31 **Italian Town**
   1928 P6 (66) Italienische Stadt
   Watercolour on Ingres Paper
   34 x 23.5 Signed bottom left

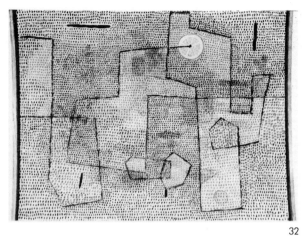

32

33

34

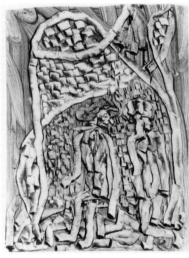

35

32 **M8**
1932.M8 (68) Emacht
Oil on cotton 50 x 64
Signed bottom right

33 **Autumn Garden Picture**
1932. W 20 (260).
Herbst-Garten-Bild.
Pastel on casein 31.5 x 47.8
Signed top left

34 **Pastor Kol**
1932 X9 (269) Pastor Kol
Oil on calico laid down on
plywood 50 x 65
Signed top left

35 **Two Women in a Wood**
1933 x 19 (259)
Zwei Frauen in Wald
Watercolour applied with a
palette knife on detail paper
39.8 x 30.8 Signed top left

36

37

38

39

36 **Head of a Martyr**
1933 Y20 (280) Kopf eines Märtyrers
Watercolour waxed on plaster
over cardboard 26 x 20.5
Signed bottom left

37 **Opened**
1933 A6 (306) Geöffnet
Watercolour waxed on calico
laid down on plywood 40.5 x 55
Signed bottom right

38 **World Port**
1933 E13 (393) Welthafen
Gouache Plaster applied with a
palette knife on Fabriano paper
43.9 x 29.6 Signed top left

39 **Struck from the List**
1933 G4 (424) Von der Liste
Gestrichen. Oil applied with a
palette knife on transparent waxed
paper 31.5 x 24 Not signed

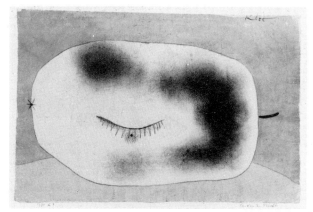

40

41

42

43

40 **The Invention**
1934 T20 (200) Die Erfindung
Watercolour, mainly applied with
spray waxed on cotton, laid down
on plywood 50.5 x 50.5
Signed top right

41 **Suffering Fruit**
1934 K7 (27) Leidende Frucht
Watercolour and oil, pen on
German Ingres paper 30.1 x 46.5
Signed top right

42 **Figure in a Garden**
1937 QU9 (129) Figur im Garten
Pastel on canvas 50 x 42.5
Signed top right

43 **In the Meadow**
1937 S12 (172) Auf der Wiese
Pastel on paper 29.5 x 20.8
Signed bottom right

44

45

44 Face of a Vase
1937 QU6 (126) Gesicht einer Vase
Charcoal and watercolour and
gouache on newspaper, laid down
on wood 66 x 49
Signed bottom right

45 Abstract Ballet
1937 X4 (264) Abstractes Ballett
Oil on canvas 24.7 x 53.4
Signed top right

46 The Grey One and the Coast
1938 J5 (125) Der Graue und die
Küste. Gouache on Jute
105 x 71 Signed top left

47 Menace
1938 T9 (309) Bedrohung
Pastel on unprepared Jute
39.5 x 54 Signed bottom right

46

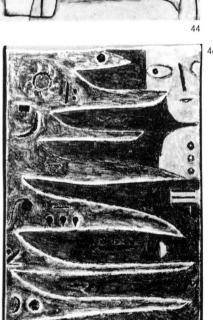

47

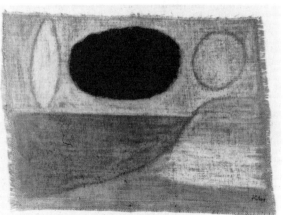

48

49

50

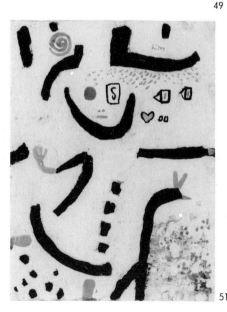

51

48 **Mother and Child**
1938 J20 (140) Mutter und Kind
Watercolour on prepared Jute
on stretcher 56 x 52
Signed middle left

49 **A Double Crier**
1939 J2 (62) Ein Doppelschreier
Watercolour on writing paper
with egg glaze
29.5 x 20.9 Signed bottom left

50 **Night is Falling**
1939 Y7 (347) Es dämmert
Watercolour on blue flag
material mounted on cardboard
68 x 50 Signed middle left

51 **A Child's Game**
1939 A5 (385) Ein Kinderspiel
Gouache and watercolour
on cardboard
43 x 32 Signed top right

61

52

53

52 **Fence and Snake Lines**
1939 (Originally untitled/Numbered)
Gitter und Schlangenlinien. Oil and gouache
on canvas laid down on plywood 56.5 x 25
Unsigned

53 **Weeping Woman**
1939 XX4 (904) Weinende Frau.
Watercolour and tempera on coloured
paper 32.9 x 20.9 Signed top left

54 **Wave Sculpture**
1939 IK8 (1128) Wellenplastik. Gouache,
Tempera and Oil and Jute 70 x 70
Signed top left

55 **Bastard**
1939 IK 12 (1132) Bastard
Paste, tempera and oil on Jute 60 x 70
Signed bottom right

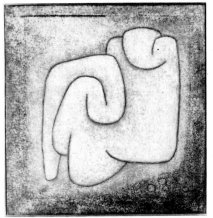

54

55

56

57

58

59

56 **Twilight Blossoms**
1940 X2 (42) Dämmer-Blüten. Wax crayon on unprepared jute on a stretcher 35 x 80 Signed bottom left

57 **The Cupboard**
1940 L16 (276) Der Schrank. Gouache on Concept paper 41.5 x 29.5 Signed bottom left

58 **Angel of Death**
(Originally untitled) 1940 Der Todesengel. Oil on canvas 51 x 67 Unsigned

59 **Still Life**
(Originally untitled) 1940 Stilleben. Oil on canvas 100 x 80.5 Unsigned

Paul Klee – history/related political and cultural events

1879 **Ernst Paul Klee born in Münchenbuchsee, near Berne. His father, Hans Klee was German, his mother Maria Frick, Swiss**

1880 **Klee family move to Berne**
The artist James Ensor (1860 - 1949) returns to Ostend to paint
7th Impressionist Exhibition in Paris

1884 **First surviving drawings in chalk by Klee**
Manet memorial exhibition in Paris
1st Salon des Indépendants

1885 The Philosopher Nietzsche (1844 - 1900) writes 'Thus Spake Zarathustra'

1886 – **Attended primary school for 4 years, followed by**
1898 **by preparatory school and then the Literarschule**

1887 American born painter Feininger (1871 - 1956) goes to Germany. Poster artist Mucha (1860 - 1939) arrives in Paris

1888 The Nabis, Brotherhood of the Symbolists, convenes in Paris. Arts and Crafts Society forms in England around William Morris

1889 Symbolist 'Revue Blanche' starts: publishes drawings and illustrations by the Nabis and such Symbolist writers as André Gide and Marcel Proust
Also publishes Strindberg, Oscar Wilde, Ibsen

1891 Swiss Symbolist artist Ferdinand Hodler (1853 - 1918) paints famous group of 3 mural paintings
Ibsen's 'Hedda Gabler' premiered in Munich

1892 Joséphin Péladan organises Salon de la Rose et Croix in Paris Its purpose 'to destroy realism and to bring art closer to Catholic ideas, to mysticism, to legend, myth, allegory and dreams.' Includes artists like Odilon Redon, Hodler
1st Exhibition of the Nabis in Paris
Munich Sezession forms, opposed to academic domination of the arts. Premature closure of Munch exhibition in Berlin – shocked by his innovative style

1893 Oscar Wilde publishes 'Salomé'
Symbolist Theatre de l'oeuvre founded – poster design by Nabis
Ibsen's 'Master Builder' premiered in Munich

1894 Rilke (1875 – 1926) writes 'Leben und Lieder'

1895 1st major exhibition of Cézanne's work, Liberal, satirical magazine 'Pan' published in Berlin, also book 'Moderne Architektur' by Otto Wagner

1896 Munich review 'Jugend' & 'Simplicissimus' appears
Alexej von Jawlensky (1864 - 1941) & Wassily Kandinsky (1844 - 1944) arrive in Munich from Russia

1897 Vienna Sezession founded by Gustav Klimt (1862 - 1918)

1898 – **Klee starts to keep diary chronicling his personal**
1901 **and artistic development. Moves to Munich, initially studying at Heinrich Knirr's private school and then at the Academy of Fine Art under Franz von Stuck with etching under Ziegler. Attends lectures on anatomy and art history, concerts and operas**

1898 First exhibition of Berlin Sezession. Nabis breaks up

1899 **He buys first box of oilpaints**

1900 **Meets 24 year old pianist Lily Stumpf**
Paris World Fair opens. Founding of the Phalanx group in Munich by Kandinsky to exhibit members work and to show contemporary art
Freud publishes 'The Interpretation of Dreams'

1901 – **First trip to Italy with the painter and sculptor**
1902 **Hermann Haller. Visits Milan, Genoa, Pisa, Rome, Naples, Positano, Amalfi and Florence Particularly liked the works of Leonardo da Vinci, Michelangelo, Pinturicchio and Botticelli, also wall paintings at Pompeii and the Aquarium at Naples**

1900 – Palazzo Castiglione built by leading Italian Art Nouveau
1903 architect Sommaruga (1867 - 1917)

1901 Beginning of Picasso's Blue Period. Exhibition at Darmstadt of Die Sieben architects
Thomas Mann (1875 - 1955) writes 'Buddenbrooks'

1902 **Returns to Berne where he continues to paint and study; reads greatly. Joins Berne Municipal Orchestra. Frequent trips to Munich, sees engravings by William Blake and Goya**

1902 Kandinsky elected chairman of Phalanx group in Munich

1903 Salon d'Automne founded in Paris. 'Kunst und Künstler' (Art and Artists) published in Berlin, promoting German artists
Thomas Mann writes 'Tristan' and 'Tonio Kröger'
Arnold Schönberg's 'Verklärte Nacht' performed in Vienna

1904 **Visits Geneva and sees paintings by Corot**
Phalanx group ends
Hesse (1877 - 1962) writes 'Peter Camazind'

1905 **First trip to Paris with friends Louis Moilliet and Hans Bloesch. Notes works by Leonardo, Rembrandt, Goya, Munch and Toulouse-Lautrec**

1st Fauve exhibition in Paris

Die Brücke 'The Bridge' forms in Dresden 'to render inner convictions . . . with spontaneity & sincerity' artists include Ernst Kirchner (1880 - 1938), Erich Heckel (1883 - 1970) and Karl Schmidt-Rottluff (1884-1976) main achievement of Die Brücke in graphic art – wood block & lino cut

Hesse writes 'The Prodigy', Richard Strauss's 'Salome' performed in Dresden. Einstein writes the 'General Theory of Relativity'

1906 **Marries Lily Stumpf. Moves to Munich Shows 10 etchings at Munich Sezession**

1907 **Birth of son, Felix. Klee stays at home, Lily goes out to work, giving music lessons. Discovers graphic art of Ensor**

Retrospective Cézanne exhibition in Paris. Brücke Exhibition at Richter Gallery, Dresden. Picasso finishes 'Les Demoiselles d'Avignon', a key work for cubism. Hermann Muthesius starts Deutscher Werkbund: an arts and crafts movement based on the theories of William Morris to fuse industry and art

Rilke writes 'New Poems'. Oskar Kokoschka's 'Murderer, Hope of Women' staged in Vienna. Schönberg composes 'Pierrot Lunaire'

1908 **Impressed by Van Gogh exhibition at Munich Exhibits 3 pictures in the Munich Sezession where impressed by works of the Marées. Exhibits 7 pictures at the Berlin Sezession. Produces glass paintings, watercolours and drawings**

Matisse founds his Academy and publishes 'Notes d'un Peintre'

The Balkan Crisis. Germany supports Austria in a dispute against Serbia.

Hugo van Tschudi sacked as Director of the National Gallery in Berlin for his 'perversive' taste in art

1908 – Factory for the AEG gas-turbine plant, Berlin, by Behrens
1909 Germany's first building in glass and steel

1909 **Views Cézanne Exhibition at the Sezession and Matisse Show at the Thannhauser Exhibits one watercolour at Glas Palast, Munich Given one of the artist Ensor's etchings, whose work he admired greatly**

Futurist manifesto published by Marinetti in Le Figaro, Paris

Neue Münchener Künstlervereinigung (New Artists' Association) founded with Kandinsky as chairman – desire to experiment without restriction. Other artists included Jawlensky, Kubin, Alexander Kanoldt, Karl Hofer

Paul Klee 1892 Berne

Paul Klee 1911 Munich (photo by Russian Author Alexander Eliasberg)

Paul Klee (Right foreground) 1900 Munich

Paul Klee 1916 Munich (photo by Paula Stokmar)

Paul Klee 1906 Berne

Paul Klee's Studio, 1920 Munich

1910 **First one man show at Berne, which then travels to Basle, Wintherthur and Zurich.**
2nd exhibition of New Arts Association which united French Cubist painters with German Expressionists
Der Sturm appears in Berlin
Die Brücke move to Berlin

1911 **Klee meets artists Kandinsky and Jawlensky, Heinrich Campendoch, Gabriele Munter and Hans Arp. Has a one man show in Munich**
Works on series of comical drawings based on Voltaire's 'Candide'. Establishes a catalogue of own works dating back to 1899. Along with Kandinsky, Jawlensky, Marc and Macke, he contributes to 'The Struggle for Art' published in Munich in opposition to the Nationalistic protest 'Deutscher Künstler' by Winner
1st exhibition of the Editorial board of the Blaue Reiter formed by Kandinsky and Marc
Takes important step towards first abstract paintings
Braque produces first Papier Collé
The Agadir Crisis. German conflict with France in Morocco
Thomas Mann writes 'Death in Venice'

1912 **Represented in the second Blaue Reiter exhibition, along with members of the Brücke. Also shows in the Cologne Sonderbund exhibition, and the Kunsthaus Zurich (as a member of Die Walze, an association of Swiss graphic artists)**
Sees exhibition of Italian Futurists at Thannhauser Gallery
Blue Rider Almanack published by Kandinsky listing aims and source material for the group
Second trip to Paris. Meets Robert Delaunay (1885 -1941), Kahnweiler, and Uhde. Sees work by Picasso, Braque and Rousseau. Translated essay 'On Light' by Delaunay into German for Der Sturm Meets Thannhauser, Meyer, Gräfe and Rilke

1913 **Exhibits in Der Sturm exhibition, Berlin, and in First German Herbstsalon.**
Kandinsky's autobiography published.
An International Exhibition of Modern Art 'The Armory Show' takes place in New York to great public and critical success
Prospect of war with the Triple Alliance (Britain, France and Russia) New army bill raises Germany's peace time strength from 663,000 to 761,000 rising to 800,000 by 1914

1914 **Assists in the founding of the Neue Münchner Sezession.Trip to Tunis and Kairouan with friends Loius Moilliet and August Macke. Discovers colour**
Werkbund exhibition in Berlin, of German Arts & Crafts Movement

Outbreak of war scatters Munich art world, Kandinsky returns to Russia
Franz Ferdinand of Austria is assassinated in Bosnia by a Serbian nationalist wherupon Austria invades Serbia and initiates the 1st World War.

1915 **Trip to Switzerland**
Macke killed fighting in France
Mondrian paints first pictures completely of horizontals and verticals
Russia and Germany are at war on the Eastern front
Kafka writes his 'Metamorphosis'

1916 **Klee called up for service. Works for airforce reserve workshop company and escorts convoys. Still paints and sees art collections**
Dada group comes into being combining artists and poets Tristran Tzara, Hans Arp, Hans Richter, Hugo Ball: Publish Cabaret Voltaire with contributions from Apollinaire, Marinetti, Picasso, Modigliani, and Kandinsky
Germany loses 281,000 men at Verdun. The Battle of the Somme from July to October cost 420,000 British and 450,000 German lives
The potato crop fails and thousands die of famine
General Ludendorff mobilises the entire civilian population

1917 Franz Marc killed at Verdun
Klee transferred to Gersthofen near Augsburg as clerk in accounting department. Meditates regularly
George Grosz, Heartfield, and Huelsenbeck form Berlin Dada Group
The United States enters the war
The Reichstag vote for an end to the war
Dada periodical published, edited by Tzara. First Dada books published, one illustrated by Janko, the other by Arp
Journal 'De Stijl' founded by Theo van Doesburg
Feininger has one man show in Berlin in Sturm Gallery

1918 **Klee demobilized. 15 drawings by Klee published in the Sturm Bilderbuch**
c. 1918 Malevitch's 'White Square on a White Ground' ultimate suprematist work
Cologne Dada Group established under journalist Baargeld and painter Max Ernst. Dada groups also in Basle and Barcelona

Russia and Germany sign the Treaty of Brest. Sailors mutiny in Kiel. November 11 Armistice. Treaty of Versailles. Kaiser Wilhelm II abdicates. Schiedemann proclaims a Republic. Eisner declares a Communist Republic in Bavaria. Spartacist Revolt led by Rosa Luxemburg and Karl Liebknecht.
Thomas Mann writes 'Reflections of a Non-political Man'

1919 **Begins to work more in oils. Work in Munich and Switzerland. Contract with Hans Goltz Gallery Munich for 3 years, later extended until 1925**

Gropius (1883-1969) founds the Staatliche Bauhaus in Weimar and publishes the Bauhaus Manifesto. Feininger and Marcks join the teaching staff.

Kandinsky made Professor of Fine Arts at University of Moscow. Schauspielhaus in Berlin radically redesigned in Expressionist tradition by Hans Poelzig (1869 - 1936)

The Communist Republic of Bavaria is defeated in elections. Kurt Eisner is murdered. Karl Liebknecht and Rosa Luxemburg are murdered. A Republican Government is set up at Weimar with Friedrich Ebert as President. The military gain political importance and crush left wing unrest

Robert Weine's innovative horror film The Cabinet of Dr Caligari shown with sets influenced by contemporary German Expressionist Art. Other important directors to emerge over the next decade include Fritz Lang (Der Müde Tode, Dr Mabuse, Metropolis) G W Pabst (Der Schatz, The Love of Jeanne Ney, Westfront, Kameradschaft) Murnau (Nosferatu & Faust) and Sternberg (The Blue Angel)

1920 **362 works exhibited at the Goltz Gallery, illustrated catalogue published in special edition of the magazine Ararat, 'Candide' illustrations published**

Asked to join Bauhaus in Weimar

1st International Dada Fair in Berlin. Dada movement spreads to Paris

The Kapp Putsch (right-wing nationalists) take power in Berlin for four days in March. Nationalists seize Bavaria. A Red Army uprising in the Ruhr is repressed by government troops

1921 **Begins teaching at the Bauhaus as a Master. During time there is Director of the stained glass workshop, the course in weaving, a painting class, and the required course for second term**

'L'esprit Nouveau' published by Juan Gris

Kandinsky founds the Academy of Arts and Sciences

German war reparations are fixed at £6,000 million to be paid £100 million annually. In March there is a Communist uprising in Saxony and Hamburg

1922 **Klee forms close friendship with Kandinsky, who with Moholy-Nagy, had joined the Bauhaus that year**

Inflation commences 760 marks = £1
Many political murders - between 1918-1922 376 political murders, 22 committed by the left, 354 by the right. Of these 18 of the left were punished, only 28 of the right
Wittgenstein publishes his 'Tractatus'

1923 **Bauhaus exhibition and Festival with 15,000 visitors. Klee's essay 'Ways of studying Nature' published in Bauhaus-Buch. Paints 'Magic Square' pictures and Theatre pictures. Spends holiday on island of Baltrum in North Sea**

Exhibits Kronprinzenpalais, Berlin

De Stijl Manifesto issued. Neue Sachlichkeit (New Objectivity) Exhibition held in Mannhiem, arranged by Hartlaub: A new group of artists disappointed, and cynical with Germany's social, political and economic problems

Le Corbusier publishes 'Vers une architechure' Magazine 'G' published in Germany by Hans Richter, Mies van der Rohe and Weiner Graefte

Inflation soars to 7,200 marks = £1, and then to 16,000,000,000 marks = £1. the French occupy the Ruhr met by only passive resistance. Hitler is imprisoned in Landsberg Jail where he writes 'Mein Kampf, part 1'
Rilke writes his 'Duino Elegies'

1924 **Founding of the Blue Four with Klee, Feininger, Kandinsky and Jawlensky 'to show how the artist's innermost desire takes shape in many ways', 1st Exhibition in U.S.A. Spends 6 weeks in Sicily where he visits archaeological sites and landscapes with historical associations**

Gives lecture 'On Modern Art' at Jena. Close of Bauhaus in Weimar

Surrealist manifesto published by André Breton, Paris

High unemployment of 2.5 million. Mark revalued one Billion paper marks = one Rentenmark. The Dawes plan gives a two-year pause in the payment of war reparations. The French withdraw from the Ruhr

Thomas Mann sells 50,000 copies of the 'Magic Mountain' Erwin Piscator founds Agitprop theatre the Revue Roter Rummel

1925 **Bauhaus moves to Dessau at invitation of City Council. Klee publishes 'Pedagogical Sketchbook'. Works by Klee included in First group exhibition of Surrealists in Paris**

Paul Klee, Felix with Fritzi the cat and Mathilde Klee 1922

Paul Klee 1924 Wiesbaden.

Society of collectors formed who guaranteed to buy at least one or two pictures by Klee a year, especially watercolours
First one man show of his work in Paris

Mondrian publishes 'Die Neue Gestaltung'
Picasso paints 'Three Dancers'

Hindenburg becomes German President. Locarno Treaty signed with Italy, Belgium, Britain and France
Alban Berg's opera 'Wozzeck' performed

Paul Klee in his studio
at the Bauhaus,
Weimar 1925

1926 **'Bauhaus' published. Moves with his family to Dessau. Holidays in Italy, visits Florence, Pisa, Ravenna and Elba**

Germany enters League of Nations
The Hitler Youth is formed for boys aged 14-18

1927 **Visits Hyères, Porquerolles Island and Corsica**

Le Corbusier builds Villa Savoye, Poissy

First Nuremburg Rally

1928 **Visits Brittany, Pont Aven, and Le Pouldin associated with Gauguin. Also visits prehistoric site of Carnac**

André Breton publishes 'Le Surrealisme et la Peinture'
Gropius resigns from the Bauhaus
Der Stürm no longer published

Brecht writes 'The Threepenny Opera'

From left to right: Wassily,
plus N Kandinsky, G. Muche,
Paul Klee and Walter Gropius
Dessau, Bauhaus 1926

1928 – **Visits Egypt: Cairo, Luxor, Karnak, Valley of**
1929 **Kings, Thebes, Assouan, Elephantine Island. Profound influence on him. Stops at Syracuse on return**

1929 **Summer visits France and the Spanish Basque Country**
Klee's fiftieth birthday marked by a large one man show in Berlin. Produces Egyptian pictures and three -dimensional studies

International exhibition of Abstract Art in Zurich. Breton Publishes Second Surrealist Manifesto (b 1904)
The Surrealist film 'Le Chien Andalou' made by Salvador Dali and Bunuel shown in Paris

Wall Street Crash in America, Economic depression in Germany

Paul Klee, Dessau 1932
(photo by Lucia Moholy)

1930 **Klee exhibition goes to the Museum of Modern Art, New York; other Klee exhibitions also in Dresden, Düsseldorf, Saarbrücken**
Spends summer in Viareggio and Engandine Produces Divisionist pictures

Empire State Building constructed by Shreve, Lamb and Harman

Wassily Kandinsky and
Paul Klee at Dessau 1930
(photo by Lily Klee)

First issue of 'Art Concret' by Theo Van Doesburg and of 'Surrealism in the service of the Revolution' magazine

4.8 million unemployed in Germany. The Young Plan negotiates lower reparations payments and the end of Allied Occupation of Germany. In the elections socialists hold 143 seats, Nazis 105 and Communists 77
Hesse writes 'Narziss and Goldmund'

1931 Offered part time professorship at Academy of Fine Art, Düsseldorf, so leaves Bauhaus. Exhibits 252 works at Kunstmuseum für die Rheinlände und Westfalen in Saarbrücken

Formation of Abstraction-Création group in Paris with Mondrian, Gabo and Pevsner

5 million unemployed in Germany

1932 Voyage to Venice, via Berne and Zurich to see big Picasso show
Summer in Hyères, St Raphael and Port Cros Islands

By October 7 million unemployed. Nazi election secures 13¾ million votes - 230 seats out of 608 securing dominance in the Reichstag. But in November election lose 2 million votes and 34 seats while the Communist gain 42 seats

1933 Enforced resignation from the Academy. Accused (erroneously) as a Jew and a foreigner by Nazis

Kandinsky moves to Paris. Bauhaus forced to close, moves to Berlin

Hitler becomes chancellor. Nazis come to power in elections 17 million votes, 288 seats out of 647. The new Reichstag empowers the governments to rule by decree for 4 years Germany walks out of disarmament conference and withdraws from the league of Nations Persecution through public book burnings and list of people proscribed for 'un-German activities' - Mann, Hesse and others leave Germany

Brunel's L'Age d'or film first shown but then banned

1934 First show in England at the Mayor Gallery, London
D. H. Kahnweiler becomes his dealer

'Art and Industry' by Read published

Hindenburg dies in August. Hitler amalgamates the offices of Chancellor and President and assumes the new title of Führer

1935 Large exhibition of 273 works at Kunsthalle in Berne which travels to Basle and Lucerne (1936). Increased reputation means he has many visitors and gives lectures. Beginning of fatal illness Sclerodermia triggered by measles

Death of Malevitch

Efrossina (Felix's wife), Felix and Paul Klee at Basle (photo by Lily Klee) 1932

Paul Klee Dessau 1933 (photo by Josef Albers)

Paul Klee Dessau 1932 (photo by Josef Albers)

Bimbo, Paul Klee, Lily Klee 1935 (photo Fee Meisel)

Paul Klee Dessau 1932 (photo by Josef Albers)

Hans and Paul Klee, Berne 1935 (Photo by Lily Klee)

Unemployment falls to one million. Germany begins a military build up reintroducing conscription and a peacetime army of 550,000

1936   **Takes cure in Tarasp and Montana in Switzerland**

Feininger returns to America

Hitler introduces a four-year plan to reduce Germany's dependance on imported goods and puts Germany on a war footing. Goering restated this as 'Guns Before Butter'. German Troops occupy the demilitarised Rhineland. Hitler negotiates an anti Comintern pact. The Berlin Olympics take place

Paul Klee Berne 1935

Paul Klee Berne 1939

1937   **Visits Ascona and Marc's widow, Maria. Picasso, Braque and Kirchner visit him. Picasso impressed by Klee's 'miniatures', later calls Klee 'Pascal Napoleon' for 'his mixture of wisdom and energy, passionate asceticism and intensity'**

Nazis sequestered 102 pictures by Klee in German Museums, included 17 in their exhibition of Degenerate Art in Munich. (200,000 visitors visited the show but only 20,000 to the official Art show)

First bar stroke pictures and tragic demonic figures

New Bauhaus founded by Moholy Nagy in Chicago. Gropius appointed to Harvard Chair of architecture. 'Plastic Art And Pure Plastic Art' essays by Mondrian. Picasso paints 'Guernica'

The Rome Berlin Tokyo Axis forms

Paul Klee Berne 1935

Paul Klee Berne 1939

1938   **Included in Bauhaus exhibition in New York, as well as other exhibitions in New York and Paris. Produces seven large panel pictures**

Kirchner commits suicide (639 works removed from museums by Nazis). Many other artists leave the country

German troops march into Austria

1939   **Spends Summer and Autumn in Lake of Moran Visits Prado exhibition in Geneva. Paints Angel series of pictures with premonition of death**

German troops enter Prague

Russia and Germany sign a ten year non aggression pact. Germany invades Poland, Britain enters the war

Paul Klee and Will Grohmann, Berne 1938 (photo Felix Klee)

1940   **Major exhibition at Kunsthalle in Zurich**

Enters Sanatorium at Orsalino near Locarno transfers to clinic of Sant'Agnese at Muralto, dies June 26th Cremated at Lugano. Funeral Service at Berne. Ashes interred in Schosshalden cemetry in Berne after the death of his wife Lily in 1946

Denmark and Norway are occupied. Germany invades Holland Belgium and France

Paul Klee Berne 1939

PAUL KLEE
A Bibliography

Chevalier, Denys	*Klee,* London, 1971
Cooper, Douglas	*Paul Klee,* Harmondsworth, 1949
Forge, Andrew	*Paul Klee,* London, 1954
Geelhar, Christian	*Paul Klee and the Bauhaus,* London, 1973
	Paul Klee, Life & Work, Cologne 1974
Giedion-Welcker, Carola	*Paul Klee,* London, 1952
	Paul Klee in Selbstzeugnissen und Bild- dokumenten, Hamburg, 1961
Glaesemer, Jürgen	*Paul Klee: Die farbigen Werke im Kunstmuseum, Bern,* Berne, 1976
	Paul Klee: Handzeichnungen I (Kindheit bis 1920), Berne, 1973. (This and the preceding volume are the first two instalments of a catalogue of the complete Klee collection in the Kunstmuseum, Berne)
Grohmann, Will	*Paul Klee,* London, 1954 (The standard monograph)
	Paul Klee, New York, 1967 (The Library of Great Painters)
	The Drawings of Paul Klee, New York, 1944
	Paul Klee: Handzeichnungen, 1921 - 1930, Berlin, 1934
	Paul Klee: Drawings, London, 1960
Grote, Ludwig, ed.	*Erinnerungen an Paul Klee,* Munich, 1959
Haftmann, Werner	*The Mind and Work of Paul Klee,* London, 1954. (One of the best of *all* books on the artist)
	The Inward Vision: Watercolors, Drawings, Writings by Paul Klee, New York, 1958
Hall, Douglas	*Klee,* Oxford, 1977
Huggler, Max	*The Drawings of Paul Klee,* Alhambra, California, 1965
	Paul Klee: die Malerei als Blick in den Kosmos, Frauenfeld, 1969
	ed., *Paul Klee Dokumente in Bildern, 1930 - 1940,* Berne, 1960
Hulton, Nika	*An Approach to Paul Klee,* London, 1956
Jaffé, Hans	*Klee,* London, 1971
Kahnweiler, Daniel-Henry	*Klee,* Paris and New York, 1950
Klee, Felix	*Paul Klee: his life and work in documents,* New York, 1962
Klee, Paul	*The Diaries of Paul Klee, 1898 - 1918,* London, 1964
	Gedichte, Zurich, 1960. (Klee's complete poems)
	The Nature of Nature, The Notebooks of Paul Klee, London 1973
	(Includes a full bibliography on Klee and a complete list of exhibitions, etc)
Klee, Paul	*On Modern Art,* London, 1948
	Pedagogical Sketchbook, London, 1954
	Some Poems by Paul Klee, translated by Anselm Hollo, Lowestoft, 1962
	The Thinking Eye, The Notebooks of Paul Klee, London, 1961
Klee-Gesellschaft, Bern	*Paul Klee, I. Teil: Dokumente und Bilder aus den Jahren 1896-1930,* Berne, 1949
Kornfeld, Eberhard W.	*Paul Klee: Bern und Umgebung-Aquarelle und Zeichnungen, 1897-1915,* Berne, 1962
	Paul Klee: das graphische Werk, Berne, 1960 (Complete catalogue of Klee's prints)

Lynton, Norbert	*Klee,* London, 1964
Osterwald, Tilman	*Paul Klee, Die Ordnung der Dinge,* Stuttgart, 1975
Petitpierre, Petra	*Aus der Malklasse von Paul Klee,* Berne, 1957
Ponente, Nello	*Klee: biographical and critical study,* Geneva, 1960
Read, Herbert	*Klee (1879-1940),* London, 1949
San Lazzaro, Gualtieri di	*Klee: a study of his life and work,* London, 1957
Soby, James Thrall	*The Prints of Paul Klee,* New York, 1945
Cologne; Kunsthalle	*Paul Klee, Das Werk der Jahre 1919 - 1933,* Cologne, 1979
Geelhaar, Christian	*Paul Klee, Life and Work,* New York and London, 1982
Glaesemer, Jürgen	*Paul Klee, Handzeichnungen III, 1937 - 1940,* Paul Klee - Stiftung, Kunstmuseum, Bern, 1979
	Paul Klee The Coloured Works in the Kunstmuseum Bern, Berne, 1979 (English edition of Glaesemer, *Die farbigen Werke ...*)
Klee, Paul	*Schriften, Rezensionen und Aufsätze,* ed. Christian Geelharr, Cologne, 1976
Klee, Paul	*Briefe an die Familie,* ed. Felix Klee, Cologne, 1979. 2 vols.
Klee, Paul	*Gedichte,* ed. Felix Klee, 2nd ed., Zurich, 1980
Munich; Städtische Galerie im Lenbachhaus,	
	Paul Klee, Das Frühwerk 1883-1922, Munich, 1979
Osterwald, Tilman	*Paul Klee, Die Ordnung der Dinge,* Stuttgart, 1975
Osterwald, Tilman	*Paul Klee, Ein Kind träumt sich,* Stuttgart, 1979
Verdi, Richard	*Klee and Nature,* London, forthcoming (Zwemmer)

General Books

Bayer, Herbert Gropius, Walter Gropius, Ise	*Bauhaus 1919 - 1928,* Museum of Modern Art, New York, 1938 London 1975
Dube, Wolf Dieter	*The Expressionists,* London 1972
Durham, Sheffield & Leicester	*Germany in Ferment,* 1970
Finke, Ulrich	*German Paintings from Romanticism to Expressionism,* London 1974
Grohmann, Will	*Painters of the Brücke,* London 1964, Tate Exhibition Catalogue
Grote, Ludwig	*50 years Bauhaus,* London 1968
Herbert, Barry & Hinshelwood Alisdair	*The Expressionist Revolution in German Art 1871 - 1933,* Leicestershire Museums, 1978
Kandinsky, Wassily & Marc, Franz	*The Blaue Reiter Alamanac,* Munich 1912, English Translation, London 1974
Richter, Hans	*Dada, Art and Anti Art,* London 1965
Roethel, Hans Konrad	*The Blue Rider Group,* London 1960, Tate Exhibition Catalogue
Vergo, Peter	*Art in Vienna 1898 - 1918, London* 1975
Wingler	*The Bauhaus,* Cambridge, Mass. & London, 1969
Willett, John	*The New Sobriety, Art & Politics in the Weimar Period* (1917 - 1933), London 1978

© Castle Museum, Nottingham 1983

ISBN 0 - 905634 - 05 - 5

Printed by Chas Goater & Son Ltd., Nottingham